WAITING ON MY RAINBOW

Waiting On My Rainbow

a novel by
Reasha Tenaye

ISBN: 979-8-21-845190-5

Waiting On My Rainbow

An Unlikely Calling (Dedication)

One day while I was at Target, minding my melanin deficient business looking for vitamins for the boys, I noticed a gentleman on the other end of the aisle. Out of nowhere, the gentleman started talking to me and complimented the boys, to which I replied the standard thank you and tried to go about my business. He then began to tell me that he has two boys and began singing their praises— what great young men they were, that one of his sons has a daughter who is his first granddaughter and more.

I'm listening, yet in my head, I feel this is so random but something in me would not allow me to wave him off and go about my business. He then started to talk about my boys, saying that they're going to be fine, they've got a great mom and they're going to go on to do wonderful things. I'm looking at this gentleman because he's older, clearly someone's Paw Paw, and I want to be respectful, but I also should be going.

As he's talking, his conversation began to shift from talking about the boys to talking about me. I remember it vividly because some of the things that he was saying were things that I had been in prayer about and asking God about at that time. I was confused but I couldn't move; it was like I was being kept there, so I stayed. He started to tell me that while I knew I was a good mom, I questioned and doubted myself when I really needed to focus on what I was supposed to be doing. He said, "you know you're a good mom, you're a good wife, you're a good person, YOU just have to know that." I looked at him like he was crazy but he, again, was confirming some really important things, so I kept listening AND I checked myself.

I wanted to cry because of where my mind was and the mental anguish I was battling. He then tells me that he's a pastor and he tell me how he and his wife have been together for decades, how she's the love his life. It was really so cute how he spoke about her. In the season I was in at the time, hearing someone speak in such a loving and enduring way about his spouse was really, really important to me.

Maybe he could see the drain on my face because he asked

could he pray with me and of course, I agreed. As he prayed for me, I could feel a shift in my mood right then and it was different; I appreciated it. The boys were surprisingly contained this whole time which was odd for them. We finished praying and I said thank you and he asked my name, which I realized we hadn't exchanged. I told him my name and he told me his. I told him to have a great day, he said, "you too" and we went opposite ways down the aisle.

The boys and I almost got to the end of the aisle, and he said, "One more thing." I turned around—goofy-grinned up because the prayer made me happy— and he said to me clear as day, "don't forget to write the book." I immediately burst into tears. He then went on to say it's a gift that God blessed him with. He said, "there are a lot of things that you know that you think other people know but they don't. You need to write the book so that they know what you know". I just cried and he was patting my back trying to get me to calm down.

I was really in shock because this wasn't the first time I received the word about writing a book. To be honest, I've been told by several people at several different times in my life that I should write a book and every single time I've dismissed it because, who am I to write a book? What remarkable things have I encountered that qualify me to write a book? Outside of emo teenage angst and my battles with self-esteem and self-worth, I'm pretty boring. This encounter, however, was really something that I just know God made happen.

When he walked away, I gathered myself and the boys were looking at me confused, trying to figure out what was going on. It was very cute that they were trying to be protective considering they were only two and three years old. I turned the corner to go ask him if he were sure that's what God Said and I kid you not, it was like he disappeared! Craziest thing ever. I went home after, you know, spending another unnecessary 30+ minutes in Target, and that conversation was still in my spirit. I prayed about it and just sat in it for the day, and it's been on my mind for the past (what?) 2 years since it happened. Life happened and I just really didn't know what to do. I've been writing and processing drastic life changes that have occurred in the two years since this meeting; I finally decided to stop being disobedient to God's plan for my life.

Thanks for your obedience that day, Pastor Ken. :)

I say all that to say this: I have no idea what this book is really going to detail. I don't know what it is going to do for anyone. What I do know is anytime in this life where I have not been a hundred percent obedient to what God has placed in me it has worked out horrendously against any good that I could have had. Reasha can do a lot but there's nothing I can do better than God so, I hope you enjoy what you read, I hope it touches your spirit, I hope you laugh, I kind of don't want you to cry but I'm not the boss of you. This book is my obedience to what God has placed inside of me and I do hope in some form or fashion that understanding what I've been through can help you locate your rainbow as well.

I want to thank God for loving me and accepting me in the midst of all of my shenanigans. If I were God, I would have kicked my butt to the curb a long time ago but that's what makes Him great.

I want to thank everyone who has supported me with this endeavor from purchasing me the software that I needed to write this book, to the experiences that have impacted my life that may be noted in this book, to those who give me words from God that He has downloaded in your spirit to share with my crazy butt, because even God knows that He created such a stubborn person that even if He were to stand in front of me and give me a Word, I would doubt it because I'm ridiculous. He uses others so that I will listen and be obedient to what's being said to me. If that isn't a loving God, then I don't know what it is.

I want to thank my sweet, sweet boys. I never thought I would be blessed to have children and God showed me favor in giving me two. They are regular blessings to my life and it's a challenge to remember what life was like without them because life with them, even in the valleys, is such a wonderful life. Bubba and Chunk, mommy loves you immensely.

I can't write a book without giving thanks and showing appreciation to my circle. Thank you to everyone who has impacted my life from the moment I first came out of my mom's uterus. Y'all are dope.

More than anything else, I thank God for being who He was, is, and always will be.

Alrighty then, let's get this party started.

√

Before We Begin…

DISCLAIMER: Sometimes we can hear, read, or watch something so ridiculous that we laugh hysterically, knowing that there is no way possible such an event(s) could happen in real life. I know this because I have thought this very thought often. Honestly, I constantly try to understand how I have yet to catch a charge. God is so abundantly great that I cannot deny His existence; His Will is why I'm not writing this book incarcerated.

We often think that things are happening TO us, when what's actually happening is we are vessels FOR someone else to be saved from a worse fate. I'm starting to understand that now because, again, the things I have lived through? I shouldn't have.

No need to beat a dead horse just yet. Know that very few situations have been changed, as well as names, to protect the raggedy; the only innocent one here is me, the victim of my own free will.

Fun fact: when I was younger, I wanted to be a can of corn when I grew up. Yes, you read that right. It's true because to this day, my mom and the rest of my family waste no time telling anyone who will listen about my prior career aspiration. Don't ask me why I wanted to be a can of corn. I mean to this day, I really like corn. Be it on the cob, creamed, street or popped, I'm here for corn.

Maybe I liked corn so much because we are the same color. Could be that we both have experience being contained, waiting on someone to free us from our can of confinement. Maybe sometimes I've been sitting around just waiting on someone to rescue me from my proverbial shelf. Or, maybe that can of corn and I connected because so many times I've gone into situations and no matter how hard I tried, the end result was me looking the same way I did upon entry.

Or maybe I was just a kid, that liked corn; that simple.

Part 1: The Beginning

I guess I'll start from the beginning.

I grew up in the only Boston that counts, Boston, Massachusetts. I was daughter number two of my mother and the firstborn of my father. Life as I know it began in a house on Roxton Street. We lived there with my Nana and Papa; Nana hailed from GA and even though she lived in Boston the majority of her life until her dying day, she always sounded like she just stepped off a Greyhound from the country.

My Papa was from Virginia. He was so amazing. He was tall, handsome and a Veteran. I loved me some him. He had gorgeous green eyes, and he had this pipe that he smoked daily. He liked this tobacco called Captain Jack: it was packaged in a white canister with black writing. While I'm sure it would be considered unhealthy now, I loved to smell that stuff. It's like it permeated through his skin and I just loved it.

My uncle also lived with us, or I guess, we all lived with them. My uncle was super cool and hung out with (or was one of) the cool guys around the way. That's all I'm going to say about that if you catch what I'm throwing. My cousin Elyse also lived there. Everyone that lived in our house was amazing, but Elyse really was. She was the pepper to my salt— truly, because that was our Halloween choice one year, dressing up as the hip hop duo Salt-N-Pepa. She was my best friend.

A proper middle child was I, sandwiched between a sister and brother. I really don't remember much about my brother from those days, except that at my kindergarten graduation he somehow managed to fall and when his head hit the ground, everyone knew it was him. That was kind of funny to me, but I guess not to him. As far as my sister, more on her later.

As a child of the '80s, I would say life was good. The era prior to smartphones and the Internet seemed so far away, even super primitive, but it was a great life. We got to play in the streets. We had home cooked meals thanks to my Nana, daily sleepovers with cousins and friends. It was truly everything. Yet, in spite of all that great, I was sad. Everyone told me about how the family dog, Kojak, died underneath my crib while I was sleeping. I believe that stupid dog left some of his mess with me.

I've always felt different and looking different didn't help much. I'm exceptionally melanin deficient as compared to the rest of my family, and I have green eyes that change colors depending on my mood. I even had the audacity to be born with golden blond hair. Two of my most popular nicknames were Blondie and Wheat Germ. My Nana gave me Wheat Germ, and when I got older and realized what wheatgerm was, I felt special, like I mattered.

I remember my sister being a typical big sister and telling me I was adopted. She would say it so often that I believed her. After all, I look so much different than everyone else that I could be adopted, right?

When we were little, my grandpa used to get lobster and he would let the lobsters actually crawl on the floor. All of us kids would scream and make noise and my grandma would always tell him to stop so we would hush, and he would... after a bit. It was really fun. As a child, my family always seemed to be so put together; I felt like we had everything. Ignorance is bliss when you're a kid, and I enjoyed basking in it.

At an early age, I questioned why I was there. I just felt different, and I didn't like it. I regularly would write my mom cards and letters apologizing for being alive. There were so many people in my house, so maybe that's why I felt that way. Those feelings of inadequacy would follow me through life. I was enrolled at the same elementary school as the rest of my siblings and cousins. There, I earned my next nickname— Chatter Cathy. As an avid reader, school came easy to me unlike most things, but it wasn't enough.

This one crazy day at school, I was in the second or third grade, and three of my so-called friends were playing with me at recess. It was a normal day, and I don't remember all of the details, but remember they started pinching me. I couldn't tell you these girls names at this point. I went in class once recess was over and told my teacher what happened. She just told me to go sit down, so I did. Oh, but when I got home, I told my mom what happened. My mom was pissed! The very next day, she stomped up the street to the school. Cussed out my teacher. The teacher tried to explain or downplay it, but my mom was not having it.

Now I may have left out the part of the story where my mom had me at 19. At the time of this issue at school, she was a mom of THREE and she did not play about her kids. (At the time of this writing, she's clearly a grandma and still plays with no one about her kids or grandkids.) I appreciated her for that because it was like she finally saw me. Those girls? I don't remember ever talking to them again.

Soon thereafter, we ended up moving. That was sad because I loved living with my Nana and Papa. When we moved, it felt like things changed in a weird way. I shared a room with my sister and my brother got his own room. It always made me mad that he got to have his own room, but then I remember he was the boy. We were girls, so we had to share. We had bunk beds, so I got over it.

Living in Mission Hill was something different. Housing project life was a new animal. We made friends with the neighborhood kids. Unfortunately, we ended up switching schools. That was terrible. I had to ride the bus to school from the projects.

I'm socially awkward. I'm young, I'm weird looking. I didn't really want anybody to bother me, yet there was this girl on the bus that just was what we would call a bully. She was younger than I was and started off being my friend, but that didn't last long. I wore glasses and had since kindergarten. One day, she just decided to bully me. I don't know why I let someone younger than me bully me, but I did. I sat there and took it; then, she took my glasses. I didn't try to take them back. I didn't cry; I just sat there like an idiot, knowing that I should say something; knowing that if she broke them, I'd get in so much trouble at home, which was only a few stops away. I just sat there, frozen.

She ended up giving them back, and I was so mad because I did nothing. I got off the bus and from where the bus stop was, my mom could see me from our third-floor apartment. I stomped off the bus with this girl who was supposed to be my friend, who just let this girl steal my glasses, following behind me. Maybe she was in on it. No idea, but I just wanted to get in the house. I got upstairs and my mom's like, "why are you walking so fast and out of breath? What's going on with you?" I was frozen again. I remembered what happened the last time something happened at school, and she went up there. I did not want that again, so I just replied, "Nothing" and went to do my homework.

Not long after our move, my grandpa would soon get sick, as he was diagnosed with cancer. That was a lot for all of us. Back then, we didn't really know what cancer was. I know I didn't. I had no idea what was going on, just that my Papa was sick. He just got really, really thin, obviously an effect of whatever treatment they were giving him at the time. I remember going into the hospital to see him. I looked at him in the bed and I was just confused because that didn't look like my Papa. My mom and the rest of the adults really did not say anything to us kids about what was going on, and it wasn't normal for us to be in "grown folks' business," so we kinda just floated in the confusion.

Eventually, he ended up coming home and there was a nurse, outside of Nurse Nana, that would come check on him regularly. He couldn't eat normal food, so there was a lot of Ensure in the house, and all of the kids grew to love those shakes. They smelled weird, but they were like a milkshake.

One night, we had gone over there to see him and we stayed really late, so we got in a cab to go back to our house. Almost as soon as we got comfortable in the bed, my mom was waking us up: my grandpa passed away. Worst thing ever in my life at that point. We rushed back to my grandma's house and he was in the bed. He looked like he was just asleep.

The ambulance and medical examiner would come to remove his body. We, my brother, sister, and I, were told to go into the living room so we couldn't see when they took him out. I remember clearly someone telling my Nana not to look, too. She did, and the noise that came out of her scared me to my core. A deep wail came out of my grandmother. I will never forget that sound for as long as I live. That sound made me cry. My Nana was a petite little thing. She didn't even really raise her voice much, and I cannot remember a time when she did. My Nana was so hurt because her man was now gone.

Looking back at that situation, I guess as a young person,

you think your grandparents are so old. My grandpa might have been in his fifties, while my grandma was a little younger, and they had been married since they were kids. Hearing her let out that shriek hurts me to this day. It's still sad to think about. Yet, in that noise, in that pain that she felt, it let me know what love was capable of; that, when you lose someone you love, it takes everything out of you. I wanted to be loved like that.

While his life couldn't continue, mine was supposed to and I couldn't understand why. I didn't want to talk to anybody. I didn't want to go to school. I loved to read but I didn't want to do that either. I just felt numb because he was gone. When we finally did go back to school, I remember my teacher gave me the biggest hug. She tried to get me back to "myself," but that Reasha was gone, and I realized it rather quickly. Death makes you grow up, and I did just that.

My growth was different. I wouldn't say I matured; I just focused on doing well at school and staying off the radar. Getting the Honor Roll was easy since I was in advanced work classes. Then, for some reason unbeknownst to me, we switched schools again. I was confused and mad but, in typical me fashion, I said nothing and did as I was told.

I was now in the fifth grade and had no identity, so I decided to mimic others. I thought I was so cool. I could copy someone's voice, I would try to copy their mannerisms— everything I could to be cool. I'm almost a preteen, so I'm weirder than normal anyway. Being weird got me to a point where I would end up in the most ridiculous situations.

There was this girl in my class I'll call "Girl A", and we were friends. There was another girl in my class, "Girl B", and I thought we were friends. We really weren't, but she was cool, and I aspired to be cool, so I followed her around to the extent I could in class and on the bus going home. I was trying to be friends with both of them, especially the cool girl because duh, I wanted to be cool. Whatever it took to be cool was what I would do at that point in my obviously oblivious young life.

During lunch, Girl B told me to go bop Girl A in the back of her head. Was that nice? Of course it wasn't. Was I trying to be cool? Of course I was. So, did I do it? Of course I did. I just walked up to the Girl A and hit her in the back of the head and stood there. Did I mention the fact that this girl was towering over me... in fifth grade?! When I tell you she got up and pushed me to the ground and stood there. I then got up and I charged at her, feeling like I was flying as I jumped up to her face and took my whole little fist and got her right in the eye! The fight was going but didn't last long. After all, we were both good students and I think this was collectively our first time fighting. I got in-school suspension, and they called my mom. Crap.

When I got home, I was concerned slightly, (just because I was used to doing things to try and get attention), knowing I was going to get a whoopin. I was prepared though: go ahead and get the belt, get the whoopin and I could then go about my business. Didn't faze me at all. I was sitting on my bottom bunk, and my mom walked in that door. She looked at me for a minute, and I just sat looking for the belt, but I didn't see it. My mom looked at me, just as calm as she could've been and said, "I am so disappointed in you." and she walked out the room.

Oh, I cried. I could have cried an ocean of tears because my mom was disappointed in me. How dare I? I'd rather take one thousand whoopins than hear my mom tell me she was disappointed in me. I hopped up and went after her, which wasn't hard in our small apartment. I tried to explain myself and she just said, "Leave me alone" and I was in shambles, like life was over. I bet you I didn't get in trouble with school again after that. A model citizen from then out.

I developed a special relationship with one of my older cousins, Denise, whom we all called Neicy. She was one of very few people in my immediate family that actually went to church. She used to invite everyone all the time and no one would go. One day, I decided to go and that was an important turning point in my life.

Going to church was fun, but being seen by someone older was more appealing to me. Neicy actually asked me how I was,

16

was interested in my nerdy hobbies and was always down to give me good advice. I loved spending time with her and her husband, who was like a father to me. My mom would let me stay over for a whole weekend sometimes, and we would go to church, just hang out and I would enjoy being seen.

One day, I read in a newspaper that the world was ending. To say I was scared would be the ultimate understatement. Not only was the world ending and I would die a child, but I was also certain beyond a shadow of a doubt that I was going to Hell. I literally cried trying to figure out how I could not spend forever burning, so I talked to Neicy about it. While I'm certain anyone else would have laughed hysterically at me, she didn't. She talked me through what I read (which ended up being a tabloid) and truly explained to me how I could avoid hell—by accepting Jesus Christ as my Lord and Savior.

While I was sold initially because I had zero interest in going to Hell, I realized that church was the only place I had been where I felt accepted, not tolerated. I was ecstatic to accept Jesus and continue my happy, now Heaven-adjacent life. I joined the youth group and children's choir (couldn't sing but they let me in), was at multiple services on Sundays and Bible study, and I tried to bring my whole family along for the ride. (Except my sister; she could burn.) I know they were sick of me, but I was on fire for Jesus, and I wanted everyone to join us in Heaven.

There was this one, life-altering night at youth group. Our youth minister passed around a mirror. She told everyone to take a moment to look at themselves in the mirror and then pass it on to the person next to you. The activity would be completed when she got the mirror back. I had no desire to spend copious amounts of time looking at myself, so I took the mirror, barely looked at myself, and passed it on. I was not in the mood for a self-esteem lesson, but I knew it was coming.

When the mirror got back to the front, our youth minister asked if everyone had, in fact, looked at themselves. Everyone lazily confirmed. She then held the mirror up and asked us to look at it. I looked at it and, just like everyone else, noticed how filthy it was because of all the fingerprints on it. She then asked, "Does everyone see the fingerprints on this mirror?"

We all shook our heads, confirming yes. What she said next still scares me to this day. "Well, this is what your body will look like if you have sex before you get married." My mouth could have hit the floor. There were gasps, there were giggles, there was crying. I was ashamed! I hadn't let anyone touch me, but I was certain that I was never going to even hold hands with a boy. Gross!

Things in my life were somewhat stable until I started sixth grade, which was crazy. There was where I met my first best friend. His name was Antonio and he cussed like a sailor; because he cussed like a sailor I, too, decided to cuss like a sailor because I, per usual, wanted to be cool. We met randomly because we both were new to the school and were in the wrong classroom. A teacher randomly walked by and asked us what we were doing and after a quick investigation, got us to our proper class. It started off me having a crush on him, and it wasn't until years later that I realized that I was not his type. By type, I mean not a boy.

Once in sixth grade, Boston Public Schools allows students to take an exam to get into one of three elite high schools. The schools were: John D. O'Bryant School of Math & Technology; Boston Latin School, which is one of the oldest and most prominent schools in the state; then there was Boston Latin Academy. Let the record show that I was a horrible test taker but since everyone else was taking the test, I had to take it too. I took the test and I got into Latin Academy, and I was super excited about it of course, because why would I not be? That was something that made me stand out and I got some attention from my mom.

Now, I want to back up here for a second because I'm sure the question of the hour is "where is Reasha's father?" We can take a quick time warp. My mom and dad were supposedly high school sweethearts. It didn't work; they got a Reasha as a consolation prize. As far as my memory served, my mom could not stand my father. I remember him coming around when I was 8 years old, and I remember that because he came to our house with some guys and my mom was so over it. I believe he brought me a pair of shoes, and I said thank you. My mom snapped, "Aren't you ask him for some money?" I just looked at him; he gave me $20, and I thought I was rich. That $20 went to my mom's hands shortly thereafter, so I never saw it again. Same went for him, because he disappeared.

Come to find out years later, we lived blocks away from each other, which was crazy. My paternal side of the family I wasn't very close with, and I felt awkward the few times I was with them. My father's brothers really tried to make up for his slack, though. This didn't happen until I got in high school, but they were awesome. They are awesome. Unfortunately for me, he, my father, was him. I remember my mom always saying, "you're just like your father" or "your father is this" and I would get so mad. I felt that she was bitter because he didn't want to be with her. I would think to myself, "he loves me and one day he'll come back around when I'm older and we'll have a great relationship." Yeah, about that… Well, we'll just finish that story later. Maybe not.

Anyway, back to this test. I passed and got into my first choice, Boston Latin Academy (BLA). I was excited. My mom took me to school the first day and, at the time, BLA looked like a university to me. Enrollment was from seventh grade through 12th grade, so I would be there for a while. As a newbie, they call you a "sixie" because you had six years to graduate. I remember nervously walking through the halls of the school, looking like a deer in headlights, and my mom just walked in the cafeteria like she owned the place. There were a ton of students there and I was whispering, "mom!" trying to get her to slow down. There was one kid mocking me and being a jerk; everyone laughed. I felt so embarrassed, but eventually I got where I needed to go and that was that.

We didn't live too far from school, but my goofy butt still took the T (public transportation) to school. I really could have walked but I was never going to go against what my mom told me to do. She said take the bus, so I took the bus. My mom gave me $0.30 to get to school and $.30 to get back and my job was just to do what I was told because I didn't want any issues. I did my best to fly under the radar. I saw my sister try to get feisty with our mom one day. That punk jumped up and got beat down. That was not going to be Reasha!

Guess it's time to rip off the bandage regarding my sister. I love my sister, always have and always will. It's always been the liking her part that has been a challenge. My sister has always been beautiful and everything about myself that I hated—my bucked, gapped teeth, flat butt, my lack of fashion sense, my awkward demeanor—my sister is the total opposite. Gorgeous, beautiful teeth, extroverted, popular with the boys and I could go on and on. Brain smarts is where I naturally excelled, but who dates someone based on the fact they read 100 books during summer reading? BOR-ING!

She's always been my standard of beauty, but I always thought that she was never a nice person unless it was beneficial for her. We were, unbeknownst to me, at war with each other. I was always feeling like it was a competition and I had zero desire to compete with anybody. Maybe it was normal sister stuff, but I was not a fan. I was just trying to stay as invisible as possible. When we did talk, we would randomly have a conversation about anything but mainly boys. I would confide in her about a guy I liked and magically, she'd date him.

There was this guy that worked at the library and, looking back, it was totally inappropriate that we liked each other. I was 16 at the time and he was definitely 23. We were friends, but he liked me and vice versa. He may have felt bad for me because I would talk to him about school and how I felt about life as we organized the shelves of the Boston Public Library (BPL). He couldn't understand why I dealt with the emotional insecurities that I dealt with.

One night at work, he had somehow gotten hold of my cellphone. He called my Nana's house and tried to explain to my sister how her mean behavior was hurting me. (DISCLAIMER: I previously alerted my mom to this issue with my sister and how I felt like she was picking on me. I don't know if my mom talked to her or not, but it was just too much.) I just knew this wouldn't end well. I don't know what he said to her, but I saw him slam the phone down and I immediately panicked. When the library closed, I walked home and knew this was about to be a thing. I just wanted to do my homework.

I got in the house, I spoke to my grandma and went in my room. I was getting my stuff together and here comes my sister. She snarled and said, "Your little friend called me" and I tried (and failed) to act confused. She started to rant and rave about how she was going to get her guy friend's sisters to jump me. I try to diffuse the situation by saying, "What is wrong with you? I'm your sister." She's still letting me have it, but I have turned my ears off because I don't respond to yelling. Again, I just want to do my homework.

She gets in my face; I ask her to leave me alone. Nana comes in the room, trying to figure out what was happening. I tell her that my sister is bothering me, and I just really want to do my homework. Nana tells her to leave but as they're walking out, my sister takes this travel sized lotion bottle off my desk and throws it at me. I promise you it was coming in slow motion. That bottle traveled so slow and ended up going past my grandma to hit me in the left corner of my chin. The second it hit me, I snapped. I jumped up, reached over Nana, I grabbed a fist of my sister's microbraids, wrapped them around my wrist, threw her on the couch, punched once, and I blacked out.

I kid you not. I don't remember anything else until Nana, aunt, my brother, and cousin were pulling me off of her. I was crazy. I yelled at her to call whomever she wanted to jump me. My whole body was hot. I was crying and I was fed up. Nana told my brother and I to go down to my cousin Elyse's house. She lived a couple of buildings down, so we went there as instructed. They asked what happened and I couldn't stop crying at that point because I was upset. Like, why would you make me do that to you? I was trying to mind my business and there she came. I thought about my mom and what happened the last time I got in a fight. I was deflated and just a ball of tears. I knew my mom would be mad at me and I would get in trouble. I was finally able to tell my cousin what happened, like who does that to their own sister? I calmed down a bit and I got up and we ran back to Nana's house. In the time we were gone, my sister packed bags; she was leaving. I later found out she went to go stay at our other cousin's house.

That was the point at which I was tired of being taken

advantage of, of people being mean to me, people not being nice. That was the day I found out that my eyes turned blue when I got angry. Lessons were learned for everybody on that day, and that carried through to school. I decided that I wasn't taking anybody's crap anymore, so from that point forward through the rest of my senior year, you could guarantee Reasha was going to be cussing somebody out because they were acting crazy. There was no calming me down anymore. I wasn't having it. I WAS NOT HAVING IT.

High school was, at the time, the truest train wreck I had had the pleasure of living through. Academically, I was DECENT, but I was nowhere near as smart as my family thought I was. I could have been better, but I was trying to be seen, be cool, be the things my sister was. I repeatedly failed.

One day at dismissal, I remember seeing this girl wearing a plaid skirt, sweater, Mary Janes and knee-high tights. As she was going down the steps, she tripped and fell flat on her face. Everyone laughed. No one asked her if she was okay. I did, and that's how I met my best friend, Patrice. We bonded over a mutual love of Green Day and Bone Thugs-N-Harmony. It was great because we were the epitome of weird Black girls, known at that time as "Oreos": black on the outside, white inside. Patrice liked anime and things like that. No idea what that was at the time because again, I was super sheltered and just not interested.

We both joined the Latin Club, professionally known as the National Junior Classical League (NJCL). Antonio joined as well, and that was big fun. During our years at Latin Academy, we ended up going to many conferences with the NJCL. My first time on a plane was when we went to Florida. We saw Chick-fil-A and we used to clown it because we didn't have Chick-fil-A in Boston. We also went to Norman, Oklahoma, and we went to a conference at UMass Amherst as well. You haven't experienced fun until you've made friends across the country due to a shared love of Latin. I took home a LOT of awards and experienced happiness and belonging. Great times.

Again, I was a late bloomer. After lunch one day, I was

sitting in Latin class, not feeling well. I asked if I could go to the bathroom. I go and lo and behold, guess what? My period decided to start. At first, I thought I was dying and somehow had been shot. When I relaxed my brain, I remembered what I learned in Anatomy class. I had no idea what to do. Again, what example? My family was the type to address things when they happen. Very reactive and not proactive. I wasn't prepared at all.

I cleaned myself up the best I could and went back to class because Ms. F would surely know what to do! I got back in class and tried to whisper to her that my period started. She said, "Well, what do you want me to do about it?" I stood there because I didn't know. She told me to go to the nurse, so I went to the nurse. She was slightly less callous and called my mom. When I got home, everyone very casually just said, "Finally! This is what you do," and that was the conversation and back to not caring about whatever crap Reasha has going on. My cycle was heavy, and I thought I was bleeding to death, only for it to stop 3 days later. Growing up continued to be a very unpleasant experience. But I guess that made me a woman, right?

So high school wouldn't be high school without a touch of drama. I guess the first bit of drama I encountered was when I was in ninth grade and I got my first boyfriend. Surprisingly, he was a football player. I was a little dorky girl in the Latin club and this very popular football player was my boyfriend. I don't even really know how the whole dating thing came about, but we dated for 3 months, starting right after Valentine's Day. (Funny story about my disdain for Valentine's Day coming later on.) We went on age-appropriate dates. He was the first boy that I kissed.

His mom was cool about him dating. I don't know if my mom cared or not. I don't even remember why we broke up, but that three months felt like forever. There were so many people at school that just could not understand why he wanted me. The popular girls were always side eyeing me and who knows what else was going on, because I was so oblivious to things of that nature. I mean, we remained friends. He ended up switching schools, so that worked out great for me because I was able to slide right on back into oblivion.

I was not popular, and I wanted to be so bad. I managed to get voted a class officer twice. I was Secretary junior year and Vice President senior year. I was also a member of TeachBoston (I wanted to be a teacher at the time). I wanted to be a cheerleader, but I just knew they wouldn't let me join because I wasn't pretty enough. I participated in many things but was not popular with the boys at all. Well, let me correct that—I was "cool" with the guys but none of them liked me in a romantic way. Looking back, I'm sure the popular girls didn't like me because I was not being fast yet was liked (in the friend way) by the hot guys at school. Goofy.

There was this guy at school that I liked from seventh grade until senior year. My friend Sharee had gassed me up to ask this clown to the prom. It took MONTHS for me to finally do it. I finally got the courage to ask this guy, also on the football team (hold up, did I have a type?!) and I was low key stalking him. He, of course wouldn't notice; if he did, he didn't care because I wasn't one of the pretty girls. I finally got the strength to ask this dude to the prom and he laughed and said no. Like, how dare I? He looked appalled that I would even take my little dorky audacity and ask him such a thing. That was crazy, but that set in motion a downward spiral of approximately ten guys telling me no.

In hindsight, I see that I wasn't the person that should have been asking anyone to the prom. That's the guy's job, but who would have even taught me how to do that? I had no examples of what men were supposed to do versus what women were supposed to do. The only decent example of a man I had died of cancer when I was in third grade. So, there's that. I was just winging it. After the fifth let down, I didn't even care because I had gotten used to being told no.

I even asked Antonio, and he totally cussed me out. He hated high school and hated people. We made a pact in sixth grade that if we didn't have anybody to go to the prom with, we would go together, and he just totally reneged on that, and I was irritated. I even asked one of my sister's friends if he would take me to the prom and he told me that he would call me back and let me know. (Hilariously enough, years later this same guy saw me after town and he told my sister that I looked good and wanted to know if I would holla at him. My response to her and him? "I'll totally give you the time of day once you let me know whether or not you're going to take me to the prom." What a jerk.

Being turned down or told no so much just makes you get to a point you stop asking for stuff. On a personal level, I had the relationship with God, but I started to feel like even He was sick of me. I was not attending church as much as I used to, though I still would pray and go to the big events. God knew the desire of my heart was to be seen, so I knew He would understand why I had to crack the popularity code rather than attend services. Maybe my rejections were my punishment for not attending services. If I couldn't do enough to make Him proud of me, should I really be shocked as to how my life was going?

Working was a decent getaway for me. Because I was young and in school, I could only work certain hours Monday through Friday. Patrice would also get a job there, so more best friend time. We had fun. To be honest, the library, surprisingly, was the filthiest place I have ever worked in my entire life. You'd be surprised what people would do to a book.

Amongst my melting pot of friends, there was a girl that I became really cool with senior year. We bonded prior to that, but when you're about to graduate you work to strengthen bonds. I confided in this girl regarding one of the Old Navy crushes of the week that I had. She told me that I should ask him out and that he likes me too, but he's shy and all this other stuff, gassing me up to talk to this guy because he and I are friends as well. I'm awkward, so I don't know how to talk to people, especially guys I like, rather well.

One day we're riding the Green Line after school because I was going to work. I notice she's being weird but I say nothing. The next day at school, she decides to tell me at lunch, my favorite time of day, that she made out with this dude. I'm LIVID. Instead of cursing her out, I got up and left the cafeteria. Now, we're not supposed to be moving about the school like this, but I was pissed. I was mad, but more hurt than anything. It was so dramatic.

She came out chasing after me, crying. She touched my shoulder, and I turned around swinging at her. She was a millisecond from catching all of the weight in my little fist straight to her jaw. I yelled, "Leave me alone!" and she stood there crying. Like, what are you crying for? You're the one that betrayed my trust. Well, her and the guy, but really her because she amplified everything involving this guy. It was then I decided that everybody is terrible.

Shortly thereafter, prom happened. She didn't even go. We had a whole debacle about our prom location 2 weeks before the actual prom. The hotel had overbooked, so we had to go with another room but got a ton of upgrades we wouldn't have been able to afford. It was a decent experience for everyone but me. I only went because I had to go.

I got paid weekly, which was kinda nice. My sister didn't work, and my mom told me I needed to give my sister my paycheck so she could get the stuff she needed for her prom, which was a few weeks before mine. My mom said she would give me the money back when it was time for my prom. Of course, that didn't happen, so I ended up having to get a cheap dress from freaking Filene's Basement that I hated. I had to have something because I couldn't not go to the prom because I was senior class vice president. My hair was terrible. I was alone (I went with the girls; shout out to my friend Sarah) and didn't get invited to any of the after-prom parties. It was a mess.

A few weeks after that came graduation time. With my other cousins, when they graduated, we would go to The Ground Round, or another local restaurant. When Reasha graduated, what did we do? Order takeout. I was so pissed, like I just kept feeling like everyone was always stepping on me and I could never have a moment. Immediately, I was like, *GET ME OUT OF HERE.* I wanted to go to college because, you know, this is the year 2000. This is all they're preaching—go to college, get a decent job, and get all the money. Really no in-between: either college or the military. I had no idea how we would pay for it because we didn't have money like that. Luckily for me, I got a LOT of scholarships and some loans, so I was able to go with no financial help from my family, who couldn't help even if they wanted to (jury was out on if they even wanted to, only because no one else had gone). I was smart, and I loved writing and I wanted to be a teacher, which provided the bulk of my scholarships for my first year. I went to an all-women's college that focused on education and I stayed on campus because I was not going to stay at home.

I was excited about it. This would be a fresh start for me. Nobody would know me there other than my roommate who went to my high school. It was going to be great. I was kissing the socially awkward, weird, unpretty Reasha goodbye. I was giving her a sharp kick in the butt and evicting her from my life because come freshman year of college, we're reinventing ourselves and it's going to be a beautiful thing.

Part 2: The College Collage

I set myself up surprisingly well for my freshman year. I had all of these thoughts on what it was going to be, and it was not that. Going to an all-women's school was great because there weren't many distractions, but I still desired to be popular and didn't know how to do it. By this time, I had a boyfriend. Yes, my second boyfriend, and he was a security guard at the library. (The other guy got deported, so this wasn't him.) Because I now lived in Cambridge, I wasn't supposed to work at the library, so I had to quit. I started working at a sporting goods store called City Sports in Porter Square, a short walk from campus.

One of the things that really pissed me off about living in a dorm with all women was that surprisingly, whenever my boyfriend would come over, everybody wanted to take a shower and come by my room. Super annoying because I lived at the end of the hall and the showers were in the middle of the hall. Bypassing the shower just to come say hi to Reasha and her boyfriend was really weird, and I did not like that. I also didn't communicate it well. No one is surprised.

I know I got on my roommate's nerves. High school brought us together but in college, I was trying to be an alternate version of myself. We were from two different cultures, and we bumped heads a lot. I guess I was really trying to figure out who I was and in trying to figure out who I was, I started not to like things about her, and vice versa. There was tension, but having the sister I had, I could deal with my roommate fine enough.

While I was a virgin, that did not mean that I did not have desires, nor I did not allow things to happen with my boyfriend. One day my roommate walked in on us sleeping. She saw clothes all over the place (I like sleeping naked) and while on the phone whispered, "Well, she says she's a virgin so why are these clothes all over the place?" I heard her but I didn't respond because I was supposed to be asleep. She grabbed some things quickly and left out. We never talked about that incident.

Then, there was the issue with the phone bill. I think I paid her for the phone bill and my check bounced or something. It was horrible. I was so bad with money back then. I would just like to take this time to apologize to my college roommate because I was not nice. I would like to blame it on immaturity, but who knows.

Academically, I got placed into a classroom because I wanted to teach middle school. I don't remember the details of how all this happened; I just know I went in that classroom with those children, and I knew within 10 minutes that that wasn't the life for me. Those kids were loud. They were obnoxious and it just was not going to work. I was trying to think of what my new plan would be because up until this point, I knew teaching was it. I was enrolled into a teaching fellows program and teaching meant my loans would get paid off. Suddenly, I'm questioning what life is because I don't want to do that anymore.

College meant electives, and I had the pleasure of taking Introduction to Sociology. That class changed my life. I realized that Sociology was amazing. I am an awkward person and people watcher, so I really wanted to understand more why people did the things that they did. I wanted to go around studying people. Maybe I'd be a psychologist. Maybe I'd be an attorney. Maybe I'd do both, but I'd figure it out later, but I knew that I no longer wanted to be a teacher.

Before I knew it, I completed my first semester of freshman year. My grades were great and I was going into second semester. January went by fine, and next up, it's February and you know what happens in February. That's right: Valentine's Day. I askedg my boyfriend what we'd do because I was obsessive and I couldn't just be surprised because I didn't like surprises. I started dating my last boyfriend (ninth grade) after Valentine's Day and having a boyfriend actually on Valentine's Day meant I actually got to celebrate it like a normal girl. I thought of all the cool things I'd get him, and he could not be less interested in anything that I talked about. I explained to him how important it was to me that Valentine's Day be great and that we did something. Valentine's Day came and I repeatedly asked him what we were doing, acting like a hyperactive puppy and completely obnoxious. In response to my obnoxious behavior, he broke up with me on Valentine's Day. ON Valentine's Day.

I did not see that coming. I was beside myself. In my dorm room, looking out the window, just in shock that he broke up with me on the phone. I went to my default, and I cried, and I cried for a really long time, and he offered no explanation, just hung up. I didn't know what to do. The next day, I had to go to work because I didn't have class. My boss, Meghan, was there and she said something small like "hi" to me and I broke down. Confused, she asked what was wrong and I told her that my boyfriend broke up with me. She felt bad (I really did not leave an option for anything else). I was pathetic, sitting there bawling my eyes out. She asked if I wanted to go home and I told her I didn't, because I needed the money. She allowed me time to gather myself since there wasn't anyone in the store at that time. I did that and I proceeded to cry about that breakup for the next three months.

He and I didn't talk. He still worked at the library, as did my best friend. She would see him and told me he just said I was "too much" and he "just could not deal." That led me into a familiar place where my dark thoughts had me believe that nobody really would love me anyway, so I didn't know why I wanted people to force love for me on this one day. If no one loved me on a random Tuesday, why do they have to love me on Valentine's Day? I kept that with me. I got over it after those three months and went back to trying to figure out who I was.

Freshman year ended and a hot New England summer emerged. While the weather was beautiful and people were out, I was working but not happy. I decided to take some time off from school because now that I wanted to major in sociology, I wanted to find another school to go to. While searching for a new school, I decided to hide myself on the internet because that was the new thing to do. I found attention on this website called BlackPlanet I had been on it since high school. I loved chat rooms. Handing out that A/S/L (age, sex, location), was invigorating. I would get messages all the time from guys telling me how pretty I was and trying to meet up. No one lived locally which was why I always talked to those guys—geographically undesirable.

One day I got a message from this guy. I don't remember what his screenname was, but we ended up exchanging numbers. His name was Jerome and he lived in North Carolina and was a trash collector for the city of Winston-Salem. I hadn't been to

North Carolina before, but the way he described it, it was very country but intriguing. He had a son but wasn't married and I thought that was odd. I told myself I was never going to date men with kids because that just wasn't my thing, so it wasn't serious initially. We hit it off quicker than I thought. We talked on the phone until the wee hours of the night and everything. He quickly asked me to be his girlfriend and I said yes with no hesitation.

One way or another, our conversation morphed into me hopping on a bus and going to North Carolina. I had my aunt and my cousins living in Raleigh, so I figured I'd go to Raleigh, and he could drive there to see me. I told my Nana I was going down there. She knew I was up to something, but she didn't really question it. I didn't tell her until the last minute because you know, I didn't think anybody cared, but I don't think she knew I was that goofy to go see a boy. I was doing all types of reckless stuff. Like, who just leaves their home and goes and meets somebody off the internet? Reasha, that's who, and I had no idea about possibly getting kidnapped; that wasn't even in my brain. I was that naive. He was who he said he was, thank God. He took me to Krispy Kreme and got me some donuts as well as a tour of UNC-Greensboro.

I went back home just knowing I was in love. I made a few more sporadic trips to North Carolina. Nana was not pleased but she also didn't judge. (If so, she did it to everyone but me like the respectable Southern woman she was.) One trip, Jerome and I were hugged up in his car, coming from who knows where, and my cousin Candice was with us. He was tired but wanted me right up under him in the front seat, and I wanted to be there. He almost fell asleep, awakened only by the safety marks on the highway. Candice then decided to drive, and we moved to the backseat. There was some... inappropriate touching going on back there. (Candice, I apologize.) There was an unsuccessful attempt at an act, and I'll leave it at that for now. We got back to my aunt's house, and I went home the next day.

All jokes aside, I was still trying to figure out what life was, and my mom was being my mom. I was back living with her because I was not in school and she was being crazy, talking about curfews and stuff. I tried to respectfully tell her I was grown and, unlike her at this particular age, I had no children and I was trying to figure life out. My mom is a tough lover and I feel like she was really trying to keep me from doing goofy stuff, trying to keep me on the straight and narrow. My mom and I got an argument one day and I told her I was moving out. Where was I going? No idea, but I wasn't going to stay there anymore. I talked to my friend Tiffany who I met freshman year. She was an affluent Persian girl that had an off-campus apartment. (Think Kardashian-esque before that was a thing.) I asked if I could stay with her and she was really cool about it, so I planted myself on her floor, like an idiot. I was going to show my mom that I was able to be okay by myself, but was I?

Staying with Tiffany was cool. I will be forever in her debt for allowing me to freeload in her one-bedroom apartment because she did not have to do that. I had taken a class at Harvard Divinity School, and I really didn't have an idea of where I would go next nor what I would do. I did, however, decide that I needed to leave Boston. Things with Jerome and I started to get serious, but I didn't want to be stuck up under him all the time.

Being the special person that I was, I decided to grab a map of the United States and with my eyes closed, I would put my finger somewhere and wherever I landed, I would apply to schools in that area. Ridiculous, but when was I not? I landed on Hawaii, Arizona, Alabama, Maryland, and North Carolina. I applied to schools in each state, and I got accepted into every single one, which surprised me. Next, I had to choose which school I would transfer to.

I talked to Nana about which school I would go to. Immediately, she told me I wasn't going to Hawaii. She also told me that Arizona was too far. I really didn't want to go to Maryland, so the choice was between Alabama and North Carolina. I really thought I was going to go to Alabama. They did not give me a financial aid package and told me that I would be notified of my financial aid once I reported to the school. Now, this was 2002 and I knew there was no way that I was going to Alabama without knowing how much money they were giving me for school;

sounded like a disaster waiting to happen. I chose UNC-Greensboro (UNCG). Nana was fine with that because even if I were to get into the shenanigans that she knew I was trying to get into, there would be family close by to save me. I ended up having to take a class at Bunker Hill Community College so I could have all my credits properly transfer over.

Onward to the South for me.

I definitely had an attitude with my aunt for a long time because she would not let me use her address to get in-state tuition, because out-of-state tuition was expensive. Regardless, I packed my stuff up and moved to Greensboro, about an hour from where my aunt was, but like 20 minutes from my boyfriend. I moved down here, away from all my family.

What I thought was going to be the greatest adult decision I had made, showed to be the worst, initially. I hated it in the South. It was so quiet. There were no police sirens lulling me to sleep, no loud music, no corner stores. Crickets or grasshoppers, whatever those noisemaking critters were, saturated my inner-city ears at night. My cellphone didn't even work. Again, this was 2002: technology was not that advanced. I was so sad and homesick. I rethought my life, because why did I even come down here? This was all terrible, but I decided to stick it out because my man was here. Balance.

When I took my first psychology class, I hated it. I found out that as a therapist, you must have a therapist. I had to rethink that because I had enough mental issues and thought I shouldn't take on anybody else's. I decided I wanted to be an attorney. I just had to switch up a few classes. I was all over the place.

On weekends, I'd be at Jerome's. He'd pick me up from campus, take me to Bojangles or Church's or wherever he thought I would be happy. He didn't have money; I didn't have money; there was only so much that we could do.

I have gingerly glanced over the fact that we had sex. Mainly because I was not excited about giving up my virginity in that way. I had sex with him because he wanted to have sex with me, and he kept talking about it. One thing about me, I do not like being annoyed. I really didn't want to, but he kept pestering me about it, so finally one day I said fine, go ahead. It was not an enjoyable experience at all. Not magical, no crashing waves or unicorns. It hurt, nowhere near glamorous as movies portray it. (This was actually one of the times where I realized that movies and TV will really set you up for failure.) I just did it because he wanted to, and I hope he enjoyed it because I didn't.

After that, our relationship changed. I was trying to get the full college experience and since he hadn't been to college, we couldn't truly relate to each other. I made a really good friend, and we would go to the club all the time. That's when I found out that I was popping in the South. In Boston, I was average because there was a melting pot of international people—from Haiti, Cabo Verde, Morocco, Venezuela, Jamaica, Trinidad and more, and seeing my little light-skinned self was nothing in Boston. But oh, in North Carolina? They loved me.

I was getting attention and I liked it, which, unfortunately, caused me to not like Jerome as much. One night, after an argument, he came to my dorm. I went outside to talk to him, and he asked if I wanted to get some donuts. I screamed NO at him. Did I care about him? Yes? Was I projecting my inner unhappiness onto him and our relationship? Possibly. He was being so controlling and I could not understand why he didn't want me making friends.

He professed his love for me that night, saying he saw forever with me, that he wanted to marry me one day. I could not be bothered and asked him to take me back to my room. When he got in the car, he was visibly upset and started speeding. I asked him to slow down because I couldn't get my seatbelt on. It was like he could not hear me and just saw red. I was scared and finally screamed for him to stop, just before the car plowed into a brick wall. He immediately started crying, saying he loved me and didn't want to lose me. I had no energy because, frankly, he almost killed us. I went back to my room, thanked God for not dying, and went to bed.

He called me a few times after that, and I didn't answer. Words would not have changed anything. I was going home for Christmas break and needed a ride to the airport. Being who he was, he drove me— the ride there was in silence. As I was headed through baggage check, he called me back. I went to him, we kissed, and he handed me some money. I slept all the way to Boston and let him know when I arrived.

Being around my family made me feel good for once. Having that time to think about what happened between Jerome and I helped me realize we really weren't a good fit for each other. It crossed my mind before and I thought us being intimate would change things. You know, I would enter this matrix and be so in love. I wasn't there. I broke up with him on New Year's Eve. I called him and told him I wanted to start my new year off right and right was not with him, and that was it. I was so terrible. So incredibly terrible, but it was time to get 2003 started.

"Y'all are meeting the guys tonight, so you better have your crap together, or else."

Gotta love getting those "or else" threats from your big sisters. It was March 2003. I decided after breaking up with Jerome that I wanted to branch out more, so I decided to join a sorority. THE sorority. While I knew much of nothing about the organization outside of the fact I wanted to join, favor shined on me and, along with six other ladies, I was selected for membership.

There was a structured educational process as well as some social time, which meant meeting other potential members. Our frat brothers, well, their frat brothers, were practicing for their probate the following night and we were allowed to come meet them. They had been filling our heads up about these guys for weeks. Personally, I couldn't give a flip about going. I was ready for my own probate, but who knew when that day would come. Guess the break from structured educational time was good enough. We packed into my line sister's car, the Diva, and we were on our way.

I was more than uncomfortable meeting at that parking deck. The ground shook and I thought it would collapse. We stood there, scared to look at these guys for fear we'd get in trouble. Our dean and big sisters were chatting it up with the other brothers until they finally acknowledged us. Each brother gave us his information, which we were supposed to commit to memory. Finally, after all the niceties, were we allowed to talk to our "line brothers."

There were so many that I walked up to the one obviously looking like he did not want to be approached. Cheerfully I said, "Hey! I'm Reasha," to which I got the response of a head nod, and he kept moving.

I thought he was extremely rude. He gave no name, no return greeting, nothing. I decided I didn't like him, and I continued to greet everyone else. Before any more could be said, structured educational time began to rear its ugly head, so off we went.

The rising of the sun meant the day those boys had been waiting for finally arrived. We were allowed to go to their probate as well as the probate of our sisters at neighboring schools. These were the first probates I would ever attend, and I was happy for them, as was everyone else in attendance. A party was held for them that night at some club, and one big sister enjoyed every moment of rubbing it in our faces that we couldn't go. It was cool though; I knew our time was coming.

On April 11th, I officially became a member of the most illustrious organization of all time. Two days later, the whole campus knew who I was, and would forever be—more than a woman, finer woman number 5: Comic Relief. Probate was such a rush! I'd relive that day over and over again if I could, minus all the extra. Maybe…

In celebration of our probate, our big sisters and brothers had a DJ come to campus at lunch. It was a lot of fun. It had to be 80° outside but I had my line jacket on. I didn't care because please believe I earned those letters. Everyone kept telling me to take it off, but it was so not going to happen. It was our day.

Throughout the day, all the Greeks on campus stopped by

to congratulate us. Before I knew it, our frat and sorors from our neighboring schools stopped by. We talked, hopped, the whole nine yards. It was almost as fun as the day before, and I cherished every moment of it.

It felt good that so many people came over to embrace their newest sisters and three newest brothers. As I spoke with my sisters, I noticed in my peripheral someone dancing, with an arm full of tattoos. I've always loved tattoos but never had any of my own. When I turned to see who it was, I noticed that it was one of our brothers from across town. The first thought was about how cool of a dancer he was. He had a beautiful smile, pretty brown skin. The next thought almost knocked me down—the person I was staring at was that same, seemingly rude, guy I wrote off.

Sadly, for me, this was the beginning of the end.

Summer came and went. Before I knew it, August hit and I was back to school. Once again, like the proud neo I was, I sported my letters every. Classes kept me busy, but no matter the circumstance I always found my way to a good party. The first week in September, one of my brothers from Chi chapter told me they were on my campus promoting a party they were having on Friday night. He wanted me to meet them outside the cafeteria and since I had nothing better to do, I walked out of my dorm to sit with them. I hugged and said hello to everyone and gave my number to another brother, Allen, who would become one of my best friends.

This would be the day I finally learned the mute's name. Yep, he finally spoke to me. His name was Maleek, but he wanted me to refer to him by his nickname.

"Just call me Leek."

It was extremely hot outside, so I figured it was time for my daily Strawberry Shortcake. One of the guys wanted a drink, and since I had a meal plan with declining balance I was buying. We went into the campus store and got everything. I got an extra ice cream for this Leek character because I figured it was the sisterly thing to do, even though I really didn't like him.

When I got outside, I slipped it to him because I did not want to have to get one for everyone. He thanked me, and I sat down to chat with Allen and my other brothers. I was already beginning to enjoy them. I glanced over at Leek but quickly turned back to my conversation. That's when we had a breakthrough of sorts.

He stood swinging his arms and asked, "Reasha, do you work?"

"Ha! I wish." I had been trying to get a job since I got to North Carolina and still had nothing a year later.

"Well, we should go out some time. Like, to Applebee's or something." He was still swinging his arms, but now he was looking at the ground. Could he actually have been nervous talking to me?

I didn't think anything of it. I replied, "Sure," and continued my conversation.

Soon, it was time for them to go back to their campus. I got up and headed toward my room, but not before the never-ending hugs and goodbyes, and not before giving my number to Leek. I mean, he was offering me a free meal. Who says no to that?

That Friday, I was too ready to shake my tail at their party. I was pissed because I had nothing to wear. This was my first Chi party, so I had to look good. I ended up borrowing a shirt from my front, Sharlie and that worked out well. I got dressed quickly, but Sharlie always operated on CP time. She was ready thirty minutes later, just as our ride arrived.

The club was just down the street from campus, next door to off-campus housing. We hopped out of the car and headed to the door. Once again, we received the Greek V.I.P. status. That line was long and as soon as we walked to the door, we were in. I must admit, I thought the club would have been bigger than what it was, and I was anticipating being hot and stuffy. Either way, I was going to enjoy myself. The DJ was on point and the place was getting packed. We posted at the makeshift stage and let the fun begin.

Before I knew it, I could barely turn around. We circled the club and miraculously found our way back to the stage. It was like girls' night out. I remember one of my sisters from A&T and I were acting a fool. There were so many guys to dance with, all we had to do was "assume the position" and it was on. (To "assume the position" was merely putting your hands on the wall as if you were about to get patted down by the police.) Yeah, we were having fun.

During one of our breaks, I noticed Leek. Boy oh boy, he was looking good. He was wearing a basketball jersey just like every other guy there, but he looked better. When our eyes met, I was greeted with a smile. I blushed, but I had to check myself because primarily, I was too light to be blushing at anyone. Secondly, I didn't want him to think I was into him like that. I mean, we hadn't even talked since the other day. For some reason though, I felt something odd for him, which definitely was not me, so I had to try my best to contain it.

We exchanged pleasantries and then started dancing. I

already knew he was a good dancer, but he was really putting it on me. Several songs had come and gone while we stayed together. He stopped all of a sudden and backed me up against the wall. I was confused because I didn't know what was about to happen. Everyone stood around smiling, when half a second later... if that man was not dancing on me while doing a handstand! I had never seen anything like it. He just threw his feet up on the wall, with me in between, and went to work. I was too through, just trying to contain the instant horniness. The party ended soon after that, and I went back to my room, greeted a nice cold shower, and went to sleep.

The following night we finally talked on the phone. My cell phone was disconnected, so I had to talk on my good ol' dorm landline phone. We had so much in common as far as music likes, pet peeves and all. It was as if we were the same person, minus the visible male/female differences. I soon found out that he was originally from New York—cool points had been deducted, because Bostonians and New Yorkers typically were like oil and water. We talked about how we both were transfers into our universities, how things had been thus far in our organizations, everything. Our conversation lasted about three hours that first night, but it seemed like it had only been twenty minutes. This continued every night for a week, after which time I invited him to visit my room. He agreed.

I was so nervous to be alone with him that I had my line sister Nicole come over. I didn't know why I was acting so juvenile because I never acted like this before. When he got there, we sat and talked for a little while. Once we got on the topic of music, I put on one of my "old school" R&B CDs. He started singing while Nicole and I sat there smiling at him.

He was definitely suave, and he knew he was getting to me because he took my hand and we danced. Talk about walking on air. I had never been held like that before. At that point, I was so taken by him that I didn't even realize that Nicole was snapping a picture of us. The energy I was receiving from him was so strong; it was like destiny brought us to this point. The song ended, with the two of us once again staring into each other's eyes. This would be the perfect time for a kiss. Lord knows I was ready for it, but just as soon as I thought it,

"Yo, it's getting late, and I have an 8 o'clock class, so I'm about to head out." Talk about timing.

"Okay then. I'll walk you out." I walked him down the hall to the door, thinking that I'd get a kiss. We talked about how much fun we had, and that hopefully we could do it again soon. He left me with a tight hug and a promise he would call me when he got home. I walked back to my room slowly. I felt like a piece of me was empty with him gone. What was wrong with me?

When I got in my room Nicole was getting herself together to get back to her room. Of course, Nicole would not be Nicole if she didn't give her input on the events that had just transpired, especially with me looking like a sad little puppy.

"So, did you kiss him?" No wonder her line name was "to-Z-point."

"No, nosey, I didn't kiss him."

"But you wanted to."

"Of course I did! I really wanted to, but he didn't seem like he wanted to kiss me, so I let it ride."

She shrugged her shoulders and said, "Oh well, it'll happen. Y'all looked cute dancing.' I took a picture of it on your phone. Anyway, I'm about to go back to Tower and finish this Biology homework."

"Aight then LS. I'll holla."

I let Nicole out and then went back and sat on my bed. About two minutes later, my phone rang. It was Leek.

"Hello?"

"Hey beautiful." The blushing began.

"Hey you. What's good?"

"I was just lettin' you know that I made it home okay. I'm about to lay it down."

"Okay then. You do need to get some rest for that early class."

"No doubt. Well, I'ma holla at you, aight?"

"Okay. Good night."

"Good night."

43

I hung up the phone, picked up my cell phone and looked at the picture Nicole took. I was staring at it because I was afraid of it. I had not felt the way I thought I was feeling for Leek since Jerome. I sure as heck didn't want things to end the same way they ended with Jerome, as that was truly not on a positive note. I couldn't tell what the future would hold for Leek and me, but I knew that I wanted him to hold me in his arms and never let me go.

These visits, phone calls, and crazy emotions would continue for a month or so. We still hadn't kissed or done anything more than hug and stare at each other. I began to get frustrated because I didn't know what the problem was and being me, I thought it was my fault. I didn't know what I was doing, but it was about to change.

Leek had come over this Thursday night just as he had done on any regular night. One of my home girls, Crystal, decided to hang out with me that night. We were so bored that she went to her room and got a bottle of Pepsi, and we pulled out the bottle of E&J I had stashed in my dresser. My tolerance was nonexistent at that time so after my first cup I felt a little tipsy. Crystal was as bad as I was—that didn't matter though because there was nothing else to do that night.

When Leek called me to let him in, I tried to fix my face so that he wouldn't think that I was drunk. When he came in, he looked almost as bad as I did. He had his right arm tucked inside of his jacket, so I asked him what it was. He pulled out a Styrofoam cup with a green drink inside. Once again, we were on the same page. I introduced him to Crystal, who was pretty much asleep but woke up just enough to say hello. I told her to go to her room and go to bed. She did after assuring me that she would meet me for lunch the following day.

Leek lay on my bed while I sat at my desk drinking slowly from my cup.

"Why you babysittin'?" He smirked at me for apparently drinking from my cup too slow.

"I'm not. I'm chillin'," was all I could muster. That smile of his could make me forget my name. With that, I took the remainder of the cup's contents to the head.

"Happy now?" I slammed the cup down like I was playing a game of dominoes.

The nights were so routine. This night's listening party featured the new Tyrese CD I got earlier that day from Best Buy. We talked about Tyrese, his singing and acting career, both we decided to be mediocre. We were both drunk, the bottle was pretty much empty. Maybe it was the liquor, or maybe I just really never noticed the time he got there, but once again he was talking about leaving. I stressed every time he said he would leave. I got out of my chair and sat next to him on my bed.

"I gotta go." He didn't look at me while he spoke.

"Oh! Why? You just got here. We didn't even dance yet." I didn't want him to go and from his lack of eye contact, I could tell he didn't want to go. As soon as he sat up, I straddled him. Never in my life had I been so bold, but I was tired of all the playing around.

He mumbled, "You know I got class in the morning." He was trying his best not to touch me. It made me laugh.

"You always say that."

"I always have class." Good point.

I refused to budge. I wanted him to stay in the bubble we created, so this was my protest.

"Come on, watch out." He patted me twice on my thighs in an effort to make me do something we both didn't want me to do.

"What if I don't want you to go?"

He looked at me, and that was when it started.

The moment his nose brushed against mine I kissed him. This time, he finally stopped running from it. His kiss, the feel of his tongue wrestling with mine, carried more of an electrical current than anything I would ever live to explain. We were at it hard and every touch of his hands moving up and down my body made me purr in excitement. He laid me down and climbed on top of me, still kissing me and exploring my body. I anticipated just what I knew was going to happen next, when he stopped.

He broke from our kiss to say, "I think I better go."

There was no eye contact. I sat up on my elbows to look at him. I don't even remember taking it off, but he put his coat back on. I looked at him seductively and whispered, "Okay." I didn't move from where I was. He turned and walked to the door, but as he reached for the doorknob, he turned back to me and tasted my tongue again. Once again, it was on.

Before I knew it, we both were naked. He sucked on my neck for a while then moved on to my breasts. He suckled each one; not too soft, but not too rough. When he got to my belly, he licked around and through my belly button, at which point I went insane. I grabbed his ears and brought him over to me. I kissed him long and deep. If I could freeze frame any one moment this would be it, hands down.

After tasting the sweat beads on each side of his neck, I nibbled on his ears, running my tongue all around and inside of them. My moves were erratic at best. Deep down inside of me I knew I wanted this night to come ever since we exchanged numbers, maybe even before then. I was ecstatic that this night was finally here.

Breathing short, heavy breaths, he paused and asked, "You got any condoms?"

"Yeah, they're over there," I said while pointing to the top drawer of my dresser. He got up and proceeded to prepare for the main event.

Now, Leek definitely was not my first sexual partner, but I could have understood if he thought otherwise. As he entered me, I gasped. He took his time entering me, with long, deep strokes following. I thought I'd draw blood the way I was digging my nails into his back. I wanted to tear him apart, but all I was able to do at that time was suck on his neck and enjoy him moaning in happiness. He looked at me and I smiled, tasting his tongue again, not wanting to ever let it go.

He flipped me over and began to excite me further through getting it doggy style. I bit my pillow to try and contain my vocal levels, but it didn't work. My moans made him more aroused. There was intense lovemaking going on, and it had little to do with Tyrese singing it on my stereo. Fate had brought us to this point. The remainder of our encounter consisted of him on top of me, me on top of him, my legs bent in ways I could never have imagined, and multiple orgasms. My legs were trembling, and I could barely keep them up. I wanted him to cum for me, and he let me know that he would. A few moments later he had, and he collapsed on top of me. We stayed there, stuck to each other, trying to regulate our breathing. Ours was the best sex I ever had.

He got up and disposed of the condom then lay back down next to me. We held each other and I kissed his tattooed back repeatedly. He began to collect his scattered clothing and put everything on piece by piece while I sat there naked, enjoying the view. When he finished, he sat on the bed looking at me. He smiled.

"What?" I looked at those beautiful eyes and wanted to see what he saw.

"Nothing. Can I just look at you?"

"You can do whatever you want." I meant every word.

He just enjoyed the sight of my naked, sweaty body on the bed, and then he caressed my face. He took my comforter and covered me up and kissed me one last time before letting himself out. I continued to lay there smiling and rewinding what just happened in my head.

October 16th had just officially become my favorite day of the year.

I started on my way the next day grinning like a little schoolgirl. I couldn't fake being happy. I was glowing. I wanted to tell my line sisters and my best friend Toni, about it but I decided to keep it to myself for a few days. I still couldn't believe it happened so I doubted anyone else would. No matter what I tried to do to get my mind off of what happened I couldn't stop thinking about it. The experience had me taken and it made everything— school, job hunting, sorors—seem irrelevant.

By Monday, those same people began to figure things out. Nicole asked and I finally let it be known. She and my other line sisters were happy for me. I just recently ended a situation with a certain Kappa that went sour, so they were glad I was getting myself together.

Leek and I continued to talk every day and night. He

47

continued to visit me, and it was as if nothing ever happened. I figured I would ask him to be my date to the Crimson and Crème Cabaret in December. Since Homecoming had come and gone, I thought it would be fun since there was chill time before final exams. He was checking his email on my roommate's computer when I asked him. Even though time had passed, and we had even been intimate, I was still nervous around him.

"So, the Deltas and the Kappas are having a ball in December. Would you like to go with me?

He smiled that smile and said, "Sure."

I was so happy! I jumped on his lap and gave him a kiss. He was just making me more pleased that I met him. All of those negative thoughts I had of him before had long since faded away, and I even felt foolish for thinking them at that time. He didn't need to know about that though. What I felt we both needed to know was where Reasha and Leek were going, so I asked him the best way I knew how.

"So do you like me or what?" I know it was blunt, but I didn't know what else to say.

His look wasn't one of shock, but it seemed to be one of those looks one gives when something you know is going to come along but you just don't know when. We moved to my bed and that's where the conversation continued.

"What you mean do I like you?" Ah, playing confused. Nice.

"I mean, do you like me? I freakin' had sex with you and I never asked if you had a girlfriend, if you have kids, all that. I completely went against standard protocol with you, so I gotta play catch up."

He laughed, which made me a little uneasy. He told me that he didn't have any kids and that was a load off my shoulders. Then he got quiet, and I got scared.

"So, what about the girlfriend part?"

He took a deep breath, and finally let it out.

"I don't have a girlfriend right now, but I do have an ex and I haven't decided whether or not I want to try that again."

I was devastated. Ex-girlfriends were ex-girlfriends for a

reason, just as ex-boyfriends were ex-boyfriends for a reason. I wanted to cry. Did he not feel the same things I felt that first night, or any other night for that matter? He may have figured out that I was uncomfortable about what he said, so he poked me.

"How do you feel about that?" What did he think? That in some way I'd be excited about that crap?

"I mean," I took a moment to compose myself and replied, "I'm definitely not happy about it but that decision is not mine to make. Personally, an ex is an ex for a reason. The only thing that matters to me is what is right here."

I couldn't even look at him. No, I didn't know this girl, but I hated her then and there. She was threatening what I wanted to build with Leek, and she didn't know I existed. I wasn't mad at him in any way. He was being honest with me, and I valued that; honesty was one of those things people couldn't deal with receiving or giving and though I didn't really want it, I was glad he was giving it to me.

We sat there, holding each other, and just trying to feel each other out. I asked him if any of his line brothers knew about us, and he told me that some of them knew, just as my line sisters knew. However, there was one that was not so approving of us talking. He told me that his line brother, Kevin, thought that us doing anything was not a good idea, and that Leek should just chill out with me. Once again that instant dislike hit, and whoever this Kevin was could take the same walk Leek's ex-girlfriend needed to take.

We sat in silence for a while, just enjoying the music. In my mind, I had to work much harder to keep him, while also wanting him to put in work to see what we could be. Things were different with him, and I let him know it.

He held my face and asked, "What's so different?"

"Everything. In the way you talk to me, the way you touch me and look at me." He kissed me, and I wanted to cry.

"Especially the way you kiss me."

He stood there holding me and time stood still for a while. Should this moment end, I didn't know if we could get it back.

Composure was what I needed. He was on my mind all

day. Our daily talks soon disappeared while the visits did not occur as much. Suddenly, work and school took over all the time he had been giving to me. My heart ached for his voice and his touch. I didn't want to harass him and drive him away, so I did a number of things to keep me from thinking about him, even though nothing really worked.

One day, between my classes, I decided to send him an eGreeting. It was so cute. It was Mr. Cheeks' single "Crush On You." Self-explanatory, but I added a personalized message telling him that no matter what I was glad we met and were friends. A few days later, I got one in return, and it blew my mind.

When I opened the card, Brian McKnight's "Back At One" played in my ear.

"The basis you need to know, if you don't know just how I feel… then let me show you now that I'm for real. If all things in time time will reveal…"

Once the song ended, the screen read "YOU'RE THE ONLY ONE FOR ME." I got misty, and I couldn't even read the personalized message he sent me. I knew then and there that something great was to become of Leek and me. I just had to be patient.

We were still going to the Cabaret together, so I decided to make the most of it. I was never into wearing makeup, but I did that night. I went to the mall and got a makeover and got my hair done. Toni did my nails. She knew how much Leek meant to me and though she thought things were moving too fast, she did everything she could to make my night special.

Leek picked me up late, but I didn't let that spoil the night. He looked great and together we were the best-looking couple there. We danced and sang to each other, ignoring everyone else in the room. That annoying Kappa felt the need to impose on my magical evening, but one sharp look from me sent him on his way. As the evening came to a close, we took a few more pictures and headed out.

While riding back to my dorm I looked at the pictures of us Leek had on his phone. Perhaps it would have been better if I had just gone through the mental images in my head. I soon came across a photo of a tattoo of "Leek" on someone's leg. I didn't remember seeing that tattoo before, so I asked him where it was.

"That's not on me." Curiosity set in, but I didn't ask anything else of it. I just continued looking through the pictures until I came across one that made me ask about it. Laying on a bed, looking as happy as can be, was Leek—hugged up with some girl.

"Who is this?" I saw myself yelling it at him in a fit of blind rage, though my actual tone was at most a whisper.

He glanced off the road to look and when he saw it, he let go of the wheel. Not the best thing to do while driving along a curve in the road. Just as soon as he did this, he grabbed the wheel as if my seeing that photo was not the big deal it was. I guess I should not have asked that question while the car was moving. Whatever the case I wasn't going to ask him again.

"That's Ashley," he finally said. "That's who I was telling you about."

My first thought after hearing that was shock. I wasn't dumb. I figured out that this chick was the owner of the tattoo. That seemed like my defeat. Anyone who gets a person's name tattooed on them was a better one than me. What was bothering me was the way he said it. I didn't know if he knew it bothered me, or if his tone was just an attempt to hide what he really felt. In any event I was speechless and remained so all the way to my room.

"Well, Reash, I had fun."

"Me too." I just stared out the window.

"What's wrong?" Silence.

"Reash? What's wrong?"

"Nothin'." I really wanted to tell him, but I didn't think it would help anything.

"Okay I don't believe you, so I'll ask one more time. What's wrong?"

"Nothin.' I'm good, really."

"Alright then. Well, thanks for inviting me."

"No problem. I'll see you later." I gave him a half-smile and went to my room.

Things were spinning in a direction I didn't want them to head. Uncertainty was ruling over me, and I knew I had to get myself together. Emotions definitely consume, but maybe my emotions were hip to something I had yet to notice. My every thought was to be with him and even when this was satisfied, I would think of ways to get him to stay longer. Nothing was ever enough. Was I finally reaching the depths of obsession?

His whereabouts were all that mattered to me. If I called and he didn't answer I would react in one of two ways: if it rang several times before hitting his voicemail, I assumed he was in class, at work, or tending to fraternity business. Should his phone ring once and then hit his voicemail, I just knew he was with that girl, so I would just hang up. His failure to return a message just made me act more obsessively than before. I walked around like a zombie, with everyone on campus thinking I was online again.

I turned to Toni and my line sisters for support, but that didn't do much. They blamed me for falling too fast. For them, things were out of order and having sex is what was making me act this way. They all figured he took advantage of my like for him as a means to get some, leaving me high and dry. However, this could not be the case and I refused to believe he would do something like that to me. Each conversation I had with Leek showed me a piece of his heart—it was not forced, and it definitely was not fake. What I saw in him, he saw in me. We trusted each other completely and we had only dealt with each other a little over two months.

The thoughts, and possible reasoning, continued to swim around in my head and my heart was drowning in a sea of the unknown. Questions could not be readily answered, while some continued to swim against the current: Why me? Why had I made love to him—because that was love, right? Why did I invite him over? Why had I bought him that ice cream? Why did I look at him? Should I have resisted everything, maintaining the thoughts of him being a rude, unfriendly, speaking-impaired man, I would not have the worst case of sadness as I have now, nor would I have such feelings of psychotic tendencies. Had I never started I would be fine, just as I was before.

I also would have never been so happy. Yes, things moved fast, but that made everything seem so right. He was everything I looked for, no matter his situation. He knew the right things to say to make me smile, and I knew that he enjoyed me. He wasn't after what I could give him physically because we had only had sex that one time. Mental stimulation was what he wanted, and we shared it as often as we could. I wouldn't trade what happened for the world. I was in love with him, so any effort to excuse his behavior and to credit mine was the right way to go.

All things considered, I decided I would let Leek go. It wasn't like I really had him, but I thought of him as a part of me. Releasing him would be a way to get myself back. I lived and breathed him, and if I ever wanted to make him mine completely, I needed to get back to how I was before him. His behavior could have been due to all of the outside forces telling him we didn't need to be together. Maybe he didn't really want me, and everyone was right. I didn't want to cry about it anymore whichever way it went.

Before going home for Christmas, we met up. The terms were not the best because of a situation I unknowingly put myself in, but he agreed to see me since I was going back to Boston. I prepared a package for him, including pictures from the Cabaret, a few poems I wrote for and about him and a few other things. Considering the period of our "relationship" it may have been a little excessive, but considering my feelings, I thought it was enough. He accepted it, but I told him not to open it while I was there. I was afraid of what he would say, if he would even say anything. We would just discuss things when I got back in January, but for now, I needed to be home and away from these feelings.

Christmas rush at City Sports was just what I needed. I started to develop a cold, but Nyquil knocked it right out. Dealing with all the last-minute shoppers left little time for me to think about Leek. I worked close to ten hours a day. I made enough money to get my phone back on, and even had money left over for a few presents. When I had a minute to myself, I would think of him, but I tried not to think too much for fear my mind would wander.

On Christmas Day everyone came over to my house, just as it had been every year. I was glad to see all of my aunts, uncles, and younger cousins—especially when they were bearing gifts.

Being with them was one of the only things I missed about Boston. They kept me laughing all the time, even when they were getting on my nerves. Times like this made me truly value my family. It was while I was on the phone with my cousin Denise when I noticed I had a call coming in.

"Neicy hold on a sec. I got a beep."

"Just call me back later chickie. Matter of fact, I should be there later."

"Okay, I'll holla."

I looked at my caller ID and I almost dropped the phone when I saw the picture on my screen. It was Leek.

"Hello?" it took so much to calm the shaking in my voice.

"Hey beautiful. Merry Christmas."

"Thanks. Same to you." Despite it all, I was gleaming from ear to ear.

"How've you been?"

"I've been alright. Just working like a slave and freezing with all this snow and ice."

Even though I was born and raised in Boston I despised being cold. I would get angry just thinking about going anywhere in the snow, or sleet, or whatever the crazy weather wanted to be on any given day.

"Aw man. I just wanted to call to tell my beautiful, beautiful, beautiful, beautiful, beautiful number five hello, and that we're so beefin'."

"Why are we beefin'?" I thought I had offended him with the letters.

"Because you didn't tell me you were getting your phone turned on."

"I sure did. You probably weren't listening."

"I listen to everything you say, and you didn't say anything about getting your phone back on."

"I told you the day I left it would be back on Christmas Eve. If I didn't tell you, how'd you decide to call me today?"

"Good point." I could tell he was smiling.

It felt so good to hear his voice. Talking to him was the best gift I had gotten that day. We talked about the things we got, the grades we ended the semester with, and how excited we were for the next semester. We talked as if nothing ever happened, and I was happy about that.

"But seriously though, not to get mushy or anything, but I really miss you Reash." My heart fluttered.

"I miss you too." He would never know the half.

"It's not the same down here without seeing you or talking to you every day. When you comin' back?"

"Hopefully on the 10th or the 11th but that all depends on my mom getting my flight booked." Hell, I'd leave right then if I could see him.

"Well, that's what's up. I don't wanna hold you because I know you wanna spend time with your fam, so I'll holla at you."

For the first time I didn't stress. Just a calm, "Okay then. I'll talk to you soon."

"Alright then. Bye, Reash."

"Bye, Mr. Taylor."

I hung up the phone proud that I hadn't freaked out, or worse, blurted anything crazy to him. The last thing I needed to do was add "I love you" to the mix. That would only complicate things further. I patted myself on the back and continued to celebrate my holiday— free from worries, stress, and Leek.

I was sad to leave Boston and my family, but I was happy to start a new year and a new semester. The break had been good to me, and I went back to Greensboro refreshed. The first day of classes went well, and I had a good time catching up with everyone. My sorority's Founder's Day was coming up and this year the three city chapters had a joint program. It was better since we all ended up at our sister chapter's program anyway.

Aside from the speaker fainting, the program was lovely. At the closing of the program the visiting Greeks and other chapters paid their respects to us all and gave gifts to our sorors. When Chi came to speak Leek would be chosen as their speaker. I hadn't talked to him since Christmas, though I called him several times. I tried not to look in his direction, but even when I took a quick glance toward the podium, we made eye contact. They way he spoke made me think he was talking directly to me. I turned my head and pretended to look at my program.

While we ate, my line sister Tameka asked me if I was going to Chi's "Sleepout for the Homeless" event after we ate. I told her I probably would and continued talking to everyone. While Allen and I were laughing about one of the soror's singing capabilities I felt a tap on my shoulder. I already knew who it was before I turned around.

"Reash." I don't know why he never just called me Reasha.

"Hey Maleek." That was the end of the conversation. I walked away and continued talking to Allen.

It was cold outside, but these fools were really putting boxes together and making "condos." I was humored by all the creativity. Rell, Alex and TJ had "central heating" in theirs, which was just a bunch of candles. I told them to be careful that the boxes didn't burn down and moved on to laughing at everyone else. There were a lot of people out supporting Chi, so it was easier to dodge Leek than normal. These geniuses were apparently trying to get the homeless drunk thing going on because they were all getting drunk. I was laughing because the main excuse given was to keep warm. That was my Chi.

One thing I learned quickly about Leek was that he was always in complete knowledge of what was around him. Each time I tried to ignore him or act like he wasn't there, he saw. He was standing on the fountain when he yelled at me.

"Hey Reasha." His drunk self, with his eyes extra glossy.

"Hi Leek."

"So, you don't rock with me anymore?"

"What are you talking about Leek?"

"You know what I'm talkin' about. You walked by me three times and ain't say a thing."

I tried to ignore him, but he started getting loud. I was so embarrassed.

He shouted, "Reasha don't love me anymore! She don't call me and she didn't wish me happy Founder's Day!"

He was really acting up and I wanted him to calm down. The funny thing about it was that everyone out there looked at me like I was the crazy one, like I drove him to that. I stood looking back at them all like they needed to get a grip, while they just let him stay there, and I stood in shock watching.

Eventually he got himself together. I guess I had not been paying attention to him for a time because he sat talking to my ace Michelle. She pulled me to the side later and told me what they were talking about. I already knew it had to be me, but I just wanted to know what bizarre things Michelle could have said to him and even more, his response. He was gone, so she told me what went down.

"I asked Leek if he had a girlfriend."

"Well? What did he say?" I was anxious because things could have changed since I left, and I was prepared for that.

"Mich then continued, "He said no, so I said, 'What's up with you and my line sister'?"

"Oh my God Mich!"

"Oh, calm down. He said he liked you and that you were really cool."

"Okay, I already knew that." I thought he was going to say something profound. This conversation wasn't helping me any.

"So, then I asked him what the problem was." Bingo: now my interest was piqued.

"He said that you're mad cool and all that, but you live in Boston and he lives here."

I rolled my eyes, frustrated and annoyed. That was an excuse considering I was in Greensboro way more than I was ever in Boston at this point. I was too through. That didn't seem like an issue before. I thought it was some bull, so I gave up. I know I said it before, but he was just making petty excuses now, and I was insulted by that. He definitely was not the only dude in Chi trying to holla, so it was nothing. By this time, I was getting sick of being lonely and since he wasn't trying to apply for the position, I was moving on.

A little after 3AM I got sleep and wanted to go home, so my line sister Ebony drove me home. I went back to campus not angry or sad—just in a mood. When I'd wake up the next day, it would be a fresh start.

On New Year's, I decided that I would be celibate. I didn't think it would be easy because I love sex, but I knew that it would be good because I could tear myself from Leek and get to know myself better. Especially when he started going off about me being from Boston... yeah, that just turned me off from him. I was doing such a great job, even though I thought about it all the time.

Our friendship was still special to me, but interactions were restricted to few emails and text messages. He was into schoolwork and so was I, but Greek business was about to take over much of our night lives. I said I'd start seeing other people, but I didn't want to, so I continued to play it solo. My intentions were not to wait for him; I just wasn't in the mood to express myself to anyone else.

On February 13th, Leek and I spent some time together. It was weird because it came out of nowhere but considering it had been a while, I didn't mind at all. He came over to my room and we caught up. It felt so good to just sit and enjoy each other. Since Leek had not attended my probate, I put in the video, and we watched what I still call to this day "The Greatest Show on Earth." I could tell he was enjoying it. I left the room when my intro was coming. I hated it, but everyone else thought it was cute. Once the video was over, I came back, and we started talking again.

I'm not sure when we stopped talking, but I knew that a split second after I turned the TV off, we were all over each other. It happened so fast. I told him how much I missed him, and he told me the same. At any other point, I would have torn his clothes off and it would have been a wrap then and there. This time, while he kissed me down to my belly button and started to unbutton my jeans, I told him to stop.

When I heard myself say it, I had to make sure that I wasn't just imagining it. Part of me thought, "Girl, what the heck are you doing?!" while my other half smiled and said, "Good job." There was no question as to how I felt about Leek, nor how I felt about myself when I was with him, but something needed to change. I wanted every inch of him and though I had him physically where I really wanted him, I needed to have more than that. I was in love with him, and I wanted him to be in love with me too, but that wouldn't happen if I opened my legs to him every time he came around. Lord knows it was hard, but I had to stick to it.

He looked up at me, and at that moment, I felt he had just heard every thought I just had. He got up, not mad or confused, but like he understood completely. We talked for a short while and then it was about that time. We kissed and I held his hand as we walked down the hall.

"I gotta stop coming over here." He rubbed his face then looked at me.

"Why?" I had an attitude about it, but that was not my intention.

"Because I hate leaving." I almost melted.

Walking back to my room, I felt glad about the choice I made. Yes, my body was on fire for him, but hell, the next day would be Valentine's Day, and we'd be together again. Just being near him was better than sex, but should I break the vow of celibacy at least it was on Valentine's Day with the man I loved.

That next day, I woke up thinking about him, and how the evening would go. I had never had a Valentine before, and I was too excited for it to be Leek.

Too bad that excitement never came.

I called and texted him about a thousand times to no avail. My voicemails went without responses. I was crushed again. I couldn't figure out who he was spending that time with, and I was somewhat relieved by that. I prayed that he was home by himself, hating the entire institution of Valentine's Day—but I wasn't stupid. I knew better. For me, the night would end at Applebee's with the rest of my single, man-hating ladies. We had a great time, but every few minutes I looked at my phone, hoping to see his number on my caller ID.

As many times before, he would resurface a few days later—this time in an eGreeting. I almost deleted it when I saw his name, but I figured he had a good excuse for not being with me on Valentine's Day. Defending him was second nature to me. What was crazy was the fact that I defended him against what could be called my better judgment. It was almost to the point where I told myself that his intentions were always good. I never did nor would do anything to hurt him so I just knew he wouldn't do anything harmful to me. It just would not make sense to me. He was just busy, which is why he sent the card instead of calling. I clicked on the link to see what he sent. While I looked at the screen, I vibed to Lloyd Banks' single "Smile."

Whenever I'm not around/ and you're feelin' down/ Let the thought of me/ be the reason you smile...

The personalized message was sweet:

"Hey beautiful,

I enjoyed the time we spent together the other day. Things have been hectic for me these past few days. Remember you are not the only one. Keep smiling."- Leek

I looped it five times because I was cheesin' so hard. I was concerned as to what he meant when he said I was "not the only one." Was this his way of telling me I was not his main girl? I would ask him about this later on, and he told me it simply meant I was not alone, and that he was there for me, even when I thought otherwise. Hell, if absence was making his heart grow fonder, why did I feel he was thinking "out of sight, out of mind"?

Whenever I wasn't with Leek, I was with my line sister Stacey. She was mocha skinned, with long black hair and she wore glasses. She was from Maryland, so I guess that's why we got along so well—we were both from the North and we shared the same bad tempers. No matter what, I knew she would hold me down and she always did. Leek's cousin, Adrian, was having a birthday party, and he and Leek invited us.

We decided to roll out there and we brought our other line sister Tameka with us. Anyway, to know Stacey and I, one would know we went to parties just shy of drunk, and we tried and get Tameka drunk in the process. The party was cool, and it was at Adrian's house which was pretty nice. Stacey was chillin on the wall, drinking her Malibu (she was on a rum kick) and orange juice, and she got me a nip of Hypnotiq and one of Hennessey, as well as a bottle of E&J from the liquor store. Before we picked up

Meka, Stacey stopped at a gas station to get gas and I got some things: Pepsi for my E&J and this Mountain Dew energy drink that I mixed with my E&J, a lovely combo that got me tipsy quick.

By the time we got to Adrian's house, we all were basically drunk. We go in there, and people are just getting there so it was straight. I finished my concoction and Leek had us drinking this Creeper he made. Come to find out there was Everclear in it and punch with soaked fruit in it, so I drink half a cup of that (well, more than half) and give the rest to Meka and proceeded to make an Incredible Hunk with my nips.

It wasn't long before I was visibly drunk, but I was chillin, holding up the wall. The DJ was on some other mess because he kept messing up "Salt Shaker" and I was getting upset. Leek came over to the wall and started grinding on me like only he could (which was arousing me). Anyway, once he was done, I was still dancing on the wall, when some girl started trying to dance with me and I pushed her away. I went and sat on Leek's lap. He thought that girl trying to dance on me was funny, but I didn't. While I was sitting on Leek's lap, I noticed all the broads in the room were staring at me sideways like something was wrong but whatever.

Since the three of us separated when we got in the house, I had no idea where Stacey or Meka went. Adrian came and told me that Meka was passed out upstairs. I got Stacey and we went to check on her. I found her in the bathroom hurling all over the place and crying about Allen, our line brother. (They started talking around the same time Leek and I did, and apparently, things weren't going so well.) I was so pissed off, but I was trying not to yell at her. We called Allen and he came and picked her up and that was that. Stacey and I agreed that Meka was banned from drinking with us for at least a year because of what she did. Stacey was pissed off, saying that Meka made her lose her buzz, but once she got another cup, she was fine.

I went back downstairs to dancing with Leek and I noticed these same girls were still looking at us. I thought they might want to start something, and I was ready for it. One broad was looking at me when I kissed Leek like he was hers or something, but whatever. He was mine.

A few minutes after that, Stacey sat in Leek's lap, and we were talking to him again. I sat my drink down, and before I knew it to my left, one broad took my drink, and to my right, this other chick grabbed Leek and almost knocked Stacey over! I almost flipped my wig!

Stacey said, "Let's go before we get arrested."

We walked out the door, and Leek followed us out. He asked what was wrong and Stacey told him what had been going down since we walked in the house. He tried to calm us down, and while he spoke to Stacey, I noticed one of those girls walk out the house, and head toward his car. I was truly about to flip then, but I tried to calm down. I told him to call me when he got home. I tried to kiss him, but to my surprise he pulled away. I thought I was going crazy. When he walked away from us, he walked to his car and let that girl in and drove off.

My mind was all over the place. But what got me was that I saw him kiss her. This was before those heauxs almost knocked my soror on the floor. That really got me. I thought I had imagined it. Man, my heart was on fire, I didn't even know what to say. Stacey tried her hardest to calm me down on the way back to campus, but it nothing worked. I was very much hurt, angry, and about forty other emotions I still cannot identify to this day.

The next day, I was still mad. Meka and Stacey told me to call him, but I didn't want to speak to him. He blatantly disrespected me, and there was nothing to talk about. From what Allen said, he didn't even remember what happened that night. I didn't believe it. Blaming it on the liquor was the punk way out, and I knew better than that. What I didn't understand was the fact that he had not even tried to call me. He knew how I felt—I'm sure Allen told him—but I guess he didn't want to deal with it. Over and over again I had to remind myself that Leek was not my boyfriend. Some tried to say I had no basis for being mad, but hell, if the shoe were on the other foot, he would have behaved the same. I just had to truly let go.

After a week or two, Leek and I started talking again. I was still very hurt by what happened, but I concluded that friendship was the best option for us. I didn't want to hear anything about that night and that's how we decided to keep it. I loved him just the same, but I could not deal with the hurt, so despite what my heart wanted, I had to do what I knew was right.

Before I knew it, I was at the gym, welcoming my newest frat brothers and sorority sisters into the Chi and Lambda chapters. I could not believe that about a year ago that was me standing where they were, revealing myself to the campus. It was great to relive those moments through the fresh fish. Now, I had ten more sisters and seventeen new brothers. Life was good indeed.

Of course, there was a party that week, and I was there in full effect. It had been a while since my last party, so I had a few drinks and headed over to this new spot called Allusions. We gave congrats to the ladies and cheered them on as they hopped. The boys would come about an hour later. Chi had adapted the principle that they need not get to their parties on time—they just had to make an entrance, and that they did. Chi was like a rowdy mass choir, having about thirty active chapter members, which did not include alums who were always around. Overall, things were great.

My chapter did our thing also with our newest party hops and all that. The party wouldn't be the same if we didn't steal the show for a few minutes. As we came through, frat cleared the way for us and cheered us on.

"Aight ladies!"

"I see you Reasha!"

"Okay '03!" Yeah, they loved us.

We moved through the crowd, searching for some sights that were just waiting to be seen. There were many, but of course, one in particular caught my eye. He wore a royal blue collared shirt, black jeans, black and blue sneakers. His Yankees hat was pulled down low, almost covering his face, but I knew well what that hat was covering. I stood at the other side of the dance floor, watching him drink and enjoy himself. I walked past and when I got close enough, I pinched him on the butt.

Leek looked at me and smiled. I knew he was drunk (that

never failed at a Chi party), but I ignored it because I knew he was proud of the boys, especially the new number five. I left him alone and continued on. We met up a few minutes later, and from that moment, I knew how the night would end. Not only was it the celebration of the Spring 2004 boys, but it was also a celebration of Spring 2003's birthday... and I had to give Leek a birthday present.

While we danced, I grinded a little harder than I normally would, and winder a little slower—I wanted him to feel me. I was definitely feenin' for his touch, and I knew he was dying for me too. It was one of the most erotic dances I had ever done. I was getting all too excited and as I danced, he put my hand on his arousal. The club was getting packed, but the heat I felt was coming from behind me. I had to stop before we got it on right there on the dance floor.

I turned and looked at him, and he whispered to me,

"Yo, you need to holla at me later."

"Aight. I'll call you when I get to my room." I had resisted him once and I didn't want to do it again.

I walked over to my sorors and then the comedy began. They must have seen us dancing and sat laughing at my face. I looked to them like I had truly just gotten some on the floor.

"Uh huh. I saw you over there dry hunchin'." Sharlie laughed, always enjoying my encounters.

"Hush girl!" I was fanning myself and trying to cool down.

She laughed. "Well, we all know what Reasha's doing later..."

There was no doubt about that. My 110-day drought was about to blow in the breeze. I figured the celibacy vow had lasted long enough and I was proud for getting that far. It had started because of him and was ending with him. Once the party ended, he met me at my room and the results were typical. Having him inside me again made me feel as great as the first time.

Something inside of me yearned for us to be unified, but something smaller yet stronger silently braced me to be hurt again.

School started to kick my butt. I had an average of two

papers due per day, and I could not handle it. There was still no job for me, so I became angry all the time. Not having money was not my style, but there was nothing I could do about it. I still had Leek and my sorors to spend time with, so I was cool.

Stacey and I were out at the plot one night, eating from Cook Out yet again. It was a beautiful night, a light breeze blowing the sticky air left over from the day. Evan, our line brother, was out with us. We were discussing the Spring '03 sleepover we wanted to have at Stacey's house the following weekend. I figured I would call Leek to see if he wanted to come. I knew he would, but I just wanted to speak to him anyway, so I called him up.

"He answered after the second ring. "Hello."

"Hey! What's up?"

"Nothin' much. What's good withchu?"

"Chillin at the plot with Stacey and E. We're gonna have a Spring '03 sleepover at Stacey's next week. You gonna come?"

"Yeah, I'll be there. Ay, Reash let me ask you somethin'."

I noticed a change in his voice, and I got a little scared, but I wanted to know what was up, so I said, "Shoot."

"If someone tried to fight one of your girls, what would you do?"

I thought that was really random, but I figured I would answer anyway.

"I mean I wouldn't just haul off and smack a chick. I'd have to get all the info on what went down first, piece it together and then act on it. Why?"

"Oh." Then he paused for a minute. I wanted to repeat my question but as soon as I opened my mouth, he hit me with the news.

"I just got in a fight." My heart dropped.

"What do you mean? Where are you? What happened?" I got frantic and almost cried.

The story was told that someone tried to jump Adrian, who in turn called Leek and they rounded up their crew to talk about what happened. Somewhere along the way, one of these other guys swung on someone and the brawl began.

"Aw, baby, you know better than that." I didn't know what

else to say. If I could drive, I would have taken Stacey's keys and tried my best to find him. I started to feel sick, like I'd throw up everything I just ate. I started shaking and sweating but I tried to calm down and be there for him.

He assured me that he was fine, but I couldn't say the same. He hung up saying he had to go. I got out of the car and told Stacey and Evan what happened. Stacey saw how upset I was and decided to take me to campus, while Evan called Leek to see what happened.

Stacey dropped me off and as soon as I got through the door I started crying. He mentioned to me that a gun was pulled— his gun. He didn't remember hitting anyone, just that it happened. What if these guys were plotting on retaliating? I could not lose him like that.

I almost didn't hear my phone ringing. I ran to it, thinking it would be Leek. It was Stacey and she was just checking on me. I told her I was still worried, so she turned the car around and picked me up to go to his house, I had never been there before that night. Clearly Stacey had, but now was not the time to discuss it.

When we got to his house he wasn't there. I called him and he said he was on his way there. I told him we were outside, he said wait for him there. He pulled up a few moments later in a car full of his so-called friends. I was already standing outside and leaning against Stacey's car.

I ran to him and hugged him tighter than I ever had before. He looked like he couldn't even believe he had just been involved in everything. We went through what happened again, and he seemed to get upset all over again.

"Leek, I understand you wanting to protect your cousin, but what's pissin' me off is the fact that from what I can tell, they only call on you when they are trying to fight somebody. Do you do the same with them?

"Hell no! I handle my own," is what he snapped back at me.

"Exactly! So why can't they do the same?" The way he looked at me proved that he was thinking the same thing.

I took a deep breath for a second before I spoke again. He

was angry and I wanted him to calm down, but more importantly I wanted him to know he was better than all this petty fighting. He often told me about his life in New York—his gang involvement, dealing, fights—and even how some of his old life followed him south. I accepted him knowing all of that, but he needed to accept his new self. These guys probably sat around all day not working but selling drugs and not taking care of their kids. Leek was in college and making something of himself. Why even associate with these people? I conveyed my thoughts to him, but he didn't try to hear me.

"You don't understand because you haven't been in this!" He started to raise his voice, so I started to raise mine.

Screw all that 'you don't understand' crap! You're in college Leek! You're running around with a bunch of wack dudes who have nothing to live for. Of course they're gonna start something over little crap. They aren't worried about you! If they were they would have waited for you. They didn't know who was in the car when we pulled up. For all they know, I could have grabbed something or someone out of Stacey's car and jumped up! Then what?"

He stood there speechless.

"Let me just ask one more thing."

He looked and said, "What?"

"Did you drive over to where these dudes were?"

"Yeah, why?"

"So, why you're trying to be everyone's Superman, you drove your all-black car with fraternity plates to somebody's house? Now, how many dudes do you know in Greensboro with a car like that? They can go to the plot looking for you or follow you home, not to mention the fact you work in the mall. So, what now?"

I didn't want to scare him or hurt him. I just wanted him to understand the severity of what happened. He just looked at me and then walked off and thought things through to himself. I allowed him that. A few minutes passed before he came over and hugged me again.

"You been cryin'?" He brushed my hair out of my face.

"Duh! I was worried about you."

"Don't worry about me. I'm good."

"Easier said than done. I can't help it. I care about you too much. You see I'm the only one out here checkin' on your crazy butt, other than Stacey."

He kissed me twice and said, "You're not the only one that cares, but I'm glad you do."

By this time Stacey had gotten out of the car and was ready to go at it with him, but I told her I thought he was cool.

"I don't care! Bro, don't you eva,' eva' do no mess like this again! Scarin' people and all that."

He smiled at her and told her everything was cool. He gave her a hug and went in the house. When I saw he was in safely, she drove off. I prayed extra hard for him that night, asking God not to take him from me just yet.

After that night, we were inseparable. Every night I went to sleep with him next to me and when I didn't, it sure felt like it. I saw things getting better for us, and I saw that he was changing. Not for me, but for himself.

One night out on the plot, he, Stacey, and I were just shooting the breeze, and talking about any and everything. That day was hot and sticky just like the previous days. I wore tan capris, a white tube top, and white flip flops. Leek was just staring at me, and I finally got sick of it.

"What are you looking at?" I hate when people stare.

"You look really nice today." It was like he was mesmerized.

"As opposed to looking a hot mess every other day?"

"You know what I mean." All three of us laughed.

He took his phone out of his pocket saying, "Let me take your picture."

"Ew! No! My hair is looking crazy!" I was letting all that thick hair of mine just roam free on top of my head and the only thing containing it was a white headband.

"You look fine. Come on." I didn't need much coaxing, so I did it. Just for him.

He sat and just looked at the phone, then me, then back at the phone.

"What?!" It was like he wanted to say something but was scared to.

"Nothin.' Can I look at my phone?"

"Okay smarty pants..."

I walked away from him and sat in his truck. I got in the driver's seat and let the seat down. I was getting sleepy. While I was in the car, he and Stacey sat on the plot, talking about relationships and all that. I was trying my best not to be nosey, and I ended up falling asleep. I was awakened by Leek shaking the car.

"Yeah, thanks buddy. I always wanted to have a heart attack at 21." He laughed, and I got out so Stacey could take me home. I gave him a hug and hopped my sleepy tail into Stacey's car.

We were halfway toward campus when Leek called me.

"Hey, Reash, you got class in the mornin'?"

"No silly. It's finals week."

"Oh, 'cause I wanted to know if you wanted to stay with me tonight."

"At your house?" In all the time we'd been whatever it was we were, I had never been to his house less for that time Stacey drove me. I hadn't been inside though.

"Yeah, that's cool."

"Aight then. Tell Stacey to bring you by the gas station down the street from the plot and I'll meet you there."

"Ok." This was random.

"So, Leek wants me to stay at his house tonight."

"Really?" Clearly Stacey knew this was coming,

"Yeah. He said meet him at that gas station down the street from the plot."

"Okay."

She drove down there, and he was waiting. I got out and hopped into his car. As we drove down the street, we were both quiet. I was confused as to what brought this on, while he seemed nervous.

"You aight?"

"I'm good."

I just sat quietly after that and enjoyed the ride. What a long ride it was. The way he called so quickly after leaving my room most nights, I thought he lived right around the corner from campus, but I was mistaken. He was taking so many twists and turns I was getting carsick.

"You been to my house before?"

"No sir."

"How'd you know how to get here that night?"

"I didn't. Stacey drove, remember?"

"Good memory. She only been here once."

His voice was shaky, but I couldn't figure out why. We pulled up to his house. It was cute. It looked really small on the outside, but once we went in, it was huge. When we entered the living room, he showed me his fish. Those fish were the biggest fish I think I have ever seen! They were tropical fish, but I swear those fish ate small animals! They were just so big. We went from there straight to his room. I was trying to be quiet, because it was late, and I didn't want to disturb anyone that was there sleeping.

His room was what I thought it would be. His walls were filled with pictures and fraternity paraphernalia. His closet was filled with clothes and shoe boxes, and more clothes. It was neater than I expected for a guy's room to be, but when was Leek not surprising me?

"Do you have enough shoes?" I joked with him.

"Nah, never enough."

He went in the kitchen and got something to eat. He asked if I was hungry, but I wasn't, so I just sat in his room watching *Midnight Love*. When he finished, he came and lay next to me on his bed. He was still acting nervous, but I just let it go. He took his clothes off and got ready to hop in the bed next to me. We slept so peacefully that night. He wrapped his arms around me, and it felt like it needed to be that way. I am not the cuddling type, nor did I like holding hands, but sometimes we make changes for the things, and people, that we love.

We had our '03 sleepover as a part of my birthday week celebration. I wanted to be in Greensboro over the summer, but I had no job and no place to stay, so it was off to Boston for me. I really just wanted to be there so Leek and I could see each other on my birthday but I had to settle for the sleepover.

Before everyone had gotten there, Stacey and I were drinking. She got me a bottle of E&J for my present, so I decided to take five shots for our founders. After that, I didn't need to drink much else. When Evan, Allen, Tameka, and Leek got there they just laughed at me. They knew it was going to happen, so they all just joined in. We played games and listened to music. Allen and Tameka left out soon because they had things to do, so the rest of us sat around drinking. I was pretty drunk and getting sleepy, so I told Leek since I was sitting on his lap.

"I need to go put on my pajamas. I'm sleepy." I couldn't even keep my eyes open. I just needed to crash on the couch.

He patted me on my thigh and replied, "Aight, come on."

He reached in my overnight bag and got my shorts and t-shirt and led me to the bathroom. I wasn't expecting him to come in with me, but it wouldn't be his first time seeing me naked, so I didn't mind. He propped me up on the sink and helped me take my shirt off. Maybe I was trying to thank him for helping me, or maybe it was the liquor, but I kissed him and slowly sent my tongue around his neck. He returned the gesture and proceeded to pull my pants off. I took his clothes off and then wrapped my legs around him. My bare body was moving quickly around Stacey's small sink. We were quiet enough that they couldn't hear us, but I'm sure they knew what was going on behind that door. Before I could look at us in the mirror I was bent over and clutching my ankles. I hit my head on the counter, and we both laughed. We paused so I could lay on the floor. He was pleasing me totally, but I needed to give him something to make him moan for me.

"Take it off." He knew exactly what I wanted, and quickly took the condom off. I instantly took him into my mouth and tasted what I loved almost as much as him. He was pleased, grabbing my hair, and playing with my breasts. This would be my first time performing oral sex on anyone and I was glad he was enjoying it. He stopped me a few minutes into it because he wanted to cum inside me. He entered me again but instead of finishing in me, he

71

released himself on my stomach. I couldn't move for the fact that I was still drunk and tired, and also the fact I had millions of Leek's children all over my belly. He helped clean me up and we both got dressed.

I stumbled out of the bathroom and passed out on the couch. I don't know what happened after that, but I knew one thing—that was the best sleep I had in a long time.

Leek drove me to the airport the day I left for the summer and that was a sad thing. I kissed him on the cheek and left my lipstick mark on his face. He was half asleep, so he wasn't very responsive to me being playful.

He gave me a hug and said, "What are we gonna do about your birthday present?"

"I don't know... mail it to me. Better yet, deliver it yourself over the summer."

"We'll see able that."

The crazy thing is, it really didn't hit him that I was leaving until he drove off. While I was checking in, he called me and said that he just realized I was going to be gone for three months and that he was going to miss me so much, at which point I started crying right there in the airport. I hate goodbyes, especially with someone that I love so much. I tried not to think about the length of time. I mean, we were both going to be in summer school and working, so the time would pass by quickly. Right?

The summer was going to be unbearable without him. It was my birthday, and I should have been happy, but I missed him so much that my special day didn't seem that special at all. He called me several times during the day, but it wasn't the same as having him there next to me. I went out to lunch with Neicy at the Hard Rock Cafe, and I felt so cool because I had never been before. After that I went walking around the city, getting familiarized with everything once again. I met up with Patrice and Antonio and we went to Starbucks and had some coffee, then I went back to Nana's house since my sister made me a cake and Nana made dinner.

Once again, the hustle of City Sports was going strong.

Leek and I talked every day, and he let me know how his classes were going. I let him know how much I missed him and how I couldn't wait to get back. It was crazy trying to go a day without seeing him every day and being in his arms night after night, but I tried to cope. One night, on a whim, I decided to text him because I wanted to know if he had been behaving himself since I had left.

"Have you been having sex since I've been gone?"

I had only been gone two weeks and I knew I could have had my itch scratched if I really wanted to, but I refused to give myself to anyone else. I just knew that he and I were going to be together and asking him was really to humor myself. I figured we both were struggling and would laugh about it later.

It was a long time coming, but his reply came: *"Yeah."*

One day I'll realize why I keep setting myself up like this. How could he? I mean, I know he's a sexaholic, but I hadn't even been gone that long, so how could he do this to me? I wasn't upset, I was enraged. I closed my phone and went to sleep, as I could not respond to that.

A few days later I got a photo mail from him. I couldn't really see what the picture was, so I texted him back asking what it was.

It's a snake wrapped around my ankle.

Oh. Well, maybe it'll bite...

I did not enjoy wishing harm on him, but it did feel good. Again, I admired his honesty, but I really didn't think Leek thought through the things he did before he acted. He texted me back asking me why I was so hostile, but again, I just could not verbalize how I felt so I didn't respond. I had to go back to Greensboro in a few weeks to take that exam, so that would be the time I would talk to him, if even then. Right now, I need to concern myself with more important things, like my family.

When I got to Greensboro I went straight to Stacey's house, and we caught up on the different things that had happened since I left. Other than her meeting a DJ and giving time to him, things were the same. She asked about Leek, and I brought her up to speed on what went down with him. The thing I have always loved about her was her ability to not take sides when it came to Leek and me. We all had the same stubborn attitude.

"Bro, you know Leek is always gonna be Leek. I don't know why you seem so surprised."

"True, but Stacey, you see how things were with us before I left. I mean, you saw what went on every night at your house. Who puts something like that to the side?"

"Speakin' of, bro, I feel some type of way about y'all doin' it in my bathroom. Was it that serious that you had to erase all that stuff I had written on the mirror?

"Reash, like, I don't understand y'all. Like, for real, because he told me about that snake text and I tried to explain to him how you would feel, but he doesn't see a reason for you to be mad."

I sighed. "Of course he doesn't see why I'm mad. Selfish people don't see anything they do as wrong."

I wouldn't say Stacey was finally taking sides, but I felt like she was not fully understanding what I was feeling. I just wanted to forget about the whole situation. I wasn't there to see him anyway.

"So, does he know you're here?"

"Not really."

"Whatchu mean 'not really'?"

"I mean, he knows I had to come back down here to take my exam, but he doesn't know exactly when."

"Well, are you gonna holla at him or what? 'Cause y'all need to talk and get things together."

I thought about it hard, but I wasn't quite sure how good of an idea that would be. True, he was the other portion of why I was so bent on coming but why should I focus on him when he clearly was enjoying himself without me? I really didn't know which way to go with it, so I slept on it. When I woke up, I sent him a text telling him I was there and that I was staying at Stacey's house, to which I got the response of "K." I let him know that I wanted to see him. We needed to talk and shift through things anyway, but I got no response. I hate text messaging.

I had a job interview at Sears the next day that ended up being a waste of my time, so I got back to Stacey's place and showered. When I got out of the bathroom, Leek was sitting on the couch. It was a shock to me, but Stacey knew he was coming over, as Leek is not one to pop up anywhere. When I looked at him, his face read that he was happy to see me yet pissed off at the same time. I knew why but I didn't want to address the issue that I knew was bothering the both of us. We said our hellos and then I went in Stacey's room as to not disrupt their conversation any further.

About ten minutes later I heard, "Reash you ready to go?" Stacey and I decided to go to the mall since I needed to get a job, and she always operated on a set schedule, so we had to move on time. This was also her way of telling me they were done talking.

"Yeah, I'm good."

I went into the living room and hugged him, and I had never felt such lack of emotion in my whole life. It hurt, but at the same time, I knew it was coming.

"How are your classes going?" I wanted to be cordial if anything.

"Fine." He wouldn't even look at me. "Aight, Stacey. I'ma holla at you."

She tried to break the silence. "Yeah, we're about to ride out too."

I was speechless. I had so much to say to him, but nothing would come out. I didn't like the way he looked at me, or not looked at me, and I really didn't like the fact that he didn't want to talk to me. Every relationship has its fair share of silent treatment, so this was our time.

We went our separate ways, but he was on my mind the rest of the day. I thought about what I'd say to him but any way I played it out the words didn't make sense. I texted him and told him I wanted to see him later, hoping we could talk everything over then, no matter how awkward I felt.

He came by around ten, as Stacey and I were watching a movie. Stacey went in her room when he got there because she already knew what was going on. He sat on the futon on the opposite end from me. We just sat there in silence for about ten minutes, looking at the TV screen but neither of us were paying attention.

He finally asked, "So how was your test?"

"It was okay, but I think I failed it."

"Why you say that?"

"Because all that was on my test was different from my study guide. I mean, even if I failed it, I'll still get a C in the class, so I'm good."

"Oh." The one-word responses were killing me.

From there it was back to silence. I just couldn't bring myself to talk about it—not because I wasn't curious, but because I didn't wanna get hurt or upset. I could usually read him well, however there was nothing coming from him… just the blank gaze at the television. Feeling at a loss, I tried what worked previously. I straddled him. He just continued looking at the screen, not moving at all.

"What's wrong?" I said.

"Nothin'." Still no eye contact.

"You sure?"

He just nodded, didn't even open his mouth to say anything. I was riding that emotional rollercoaster again, for I felt the tears welling up, but I contained them. I grabbed his face and made him look at me. Our eyes met and we looked into each other's hurt. Breaking away from the glance would have only been confirmation of guilt. I knew he was hurt by my words, but I was hurt by his actions. How would we make it right was the tricky part, so I did what worked second best; I got physical.

I kissed him. Lightly the first time to see if he would return the gesture, which he did. The second time I slid my tongue into his mouth, and he received it. The goal was not to force myself on him, nor force a discussion but just to find solace in our bubble again.

My tongue moved around his neck and soon I began to travel down to where we would both find southern comfort. Before I did, I paused to read his face, but there was still nothing.

I kissed him again, asking, "You want me to stop?"

He replied, "No," and I continued.

I lifted his shirt and kissed his tattooed body slowly and softly. I took my time because this was my way of apologizing. I licked his belly and then began to unbuckle, unbutton, and unzip, until I held him in my hands. Delicately I placed him into my mouth, and like a baby sucking on a bottle, I held on to him and would not stop until the bottle was empty.

I got up and put everything back the way I found it and laid my head on his shoulder. I went to hold his hand, I guess in an effort to see that he accepted my apology, and he opened up to me. His energy still did not tell me he was completely forgiving; just that he was aware.

"I gotta go. It's getting late."

I didn't try to stop him, I just let him leave. I didn't feel there was anything else to do. I would call him the next day, and the day after that, but he just brushed me off. I should have seen it coming that he would be unavailable my last night there, but I hoped it would be different. Whether I liked it or not, it was back to Boston and back to my solitude.

If you're wondering when I had time to go to class (because it would appear that all I did was chase this man around), I had time; I just didn't utilize it properly. While school was something that came easy for me, I didn't think myself as smart as other people did. The only classes I really enjoyed were those that were based in Criminology and African American studies. The professors in the African American Studies department were always amazing and I loved how they challenged my brain.

FUN FACT: when I enrolled at UNCG, I had the intention of studying sociology and becoming an attorney. Upon meeting with my advisor and letting him know my goals, he shattered my dreams quite abruptly. He told me that there was no way I would get into law school with a 3.28 GPA. I was floored. I really thought that I knew what I wanted and I was going toward it, and my dreams were dashed in one advising session. I didn't know what I was going to do nor what my life was going to be. About a week or so later, I decided to get a grip and realize that a professor that didn't even have tenure really was in no place to tell me what I could or could not be, and I let know that be known.

Unfortunately, the damage had been done and I really didn't know what I wanted to do with myself; enter depression. I had taken out a ton of student loans and still was short with my out-of-state tuition. I ended up not having the money that I needed in order to stay at school so, in the middle of the semester, I was kicked out. Did any of my friends know this? Of course not. I kept it from as many people as possible because I had been embarrassed about too many other things already—I very rarely had money to do anything. The whole point of leaving Boston was to reinvent myself, to be able to show myself that I could be fine in the alone I was always in. Truth is, I wasn't, and I didn't know how to fix it.

When I got kicked out of school, I ended up sleeping on the couch of some of my sorors. While people thought I was going to class, I wasn't. I literally couldn't. The plot twist here is that I had been elected the President of an organization that I loved while I was an active student, and I could not bear them knowing my secret. So, I tried to be a good president (I failed), still walked around campus, went to social events, went to parties, drank a lot. I tried to act like I was still a student. I just didn't go to class. I would hide in the library. I would do anything so that no one would see me. Oddly enough, no one asked.

I felt so lonely. It's not like I could have asked my family for money because again, they didn't have it. My uncle helped out when he could, but he couldn't be a constant donor and, honestly, that wasn't his job. My best friend cosigned on my loans, and I regretted having her do that because that wasn't her responsibility either. I surely wasn't going to go back to Boston. I was eventually able to take out more loans and was able to come back on campus, but I had to file paperwork due to ending up on academic probation because I wanted to party and drink and not face my problems.

I really don't know why I was so fixated on being cool and being seen. There was so much more to life than that, but that was not something I would have listened to at the time. Trying to keep up appearances with people who weren't even looking at you is exhausting, but that's exactly what I did. I don't know how I survived myself most days. I really thought that moving south and being around people who didn't know me was going to get me the happiness that I was craving; I was very much not correct with that. I was spiraling and didn't even know it.

When holidays came, I didn't always have the money to go home, so I would stay on campus. Some of my friends would be gracious enough to allow me to go home with them. I spent long weekends in Henderson with one family; holidays with Toni in Louisburg. I really admired my girls and envied the close bonds they had with their fathers, longing for my own. Nevertheless, I will forever be appreciative for these friends, these sisters, and how they took care of me. I really didn't even know how to take care of myself, which was crazy because I had a whole lot of pride for someone who didn't have anything else.

I somehow got funds to take summer classes, but had nowhere to live so, homeless again. Luckily, my Assistant Dean of Pledges (ADP) Nikki, let me stay with her. We had a time that summer, and I'll never forget her having my back, especially when she didn't have to. When I talk about my sorority, there really are no limits that they would not go for me and while I couldn't always explain it, I would do the exact same for them. My sorority sisters hold an incredibly special place in my heart for the way that they took care of me when my own family couldn't, or when I just couldn't open my mouth to say ask. I will forever be indebted to them. The connections are truly lifelong, and they will always hold a special place in my heart.

After what felt like a decade of courses, academic probation/suspension and getting reinstated at school, losing financial aid, finding financial aid, being homeless, all of the things, it was finally time for me to graduate from UNCG. Despite all the shenanigans going on within my personal life being in shambles, I had finally completed all the courses necessary to get my Bachelor of Arts in Sociology and African American Studies, with a minor in Communications. When it was time for me to graduate, I knew that a lot of my family wasn't going to come because economically that just wasn't something that was going to happen. I was excited to have finally finished something that I started.

My mom, Nana and sister came down for the graduation while my aunt and cousins in Raleigh also came. The weekend was going well until my sister's other personality came out. There was an attitude in her the whole time. Celebrating me was like an allergy for her. I was not sure why she even bothered coming because she looked like she was irritated to be there.

As we were leaving the Coliseum, I was in the passenger seat giving her directions and she began being really nasty to me. One thing led to another, and we got into an argument. I don't remember exactly what happened, but I remembered saying something to the effect of, "do you want me to beat you up again like I did in high school?" and she was PISSED but quiet. She dropped us off at my apartment and left, literally went straight to the airport, and flew back to Boston, leaving Nana and our mom at my house. Mind you, I did not have a license nor vehicle at this time.

I tried calling her; she would not answer. She finally picked up and I said, "what are you doing? I'm your sister," and she said in a rage, "you're my half-sister, b****!" and hung up. That was supposed to hurt, but I laughed.

Eventually one of my friends took my mom and Nana to the airport the next day. This volatile relationship with my sister just made no sense to me. I really didn't know why she was so angry. I just really wanted her to love me and be my friend, yet I could never understand why there was always an issue whenever it was time for me to shine because I had no problem celebrating her. It could have just been that she didn't like me, and I was starting to be okay with it.

That September, Nana was turning 74 and the family decided to have a big party for her. I wanted to go because I love my Nana yet financially, it wasn't possible. It was asked that my aunt in Raleigh let me ride with her because she was driving up. Her response was for me to have someone bring me to Raleigh at 3AM and then I could ride with them, as going to Greensboro to get me would be backtracking. A 3AM ride to Raleigh wasn't possible for me. I ended up missing the party and so did my aunt because she decided not to go.

I hate that I missed it, because two months later, I would get heartbreaking news. On November 2nd, 2006, I was informed that Nana had Leukemia. My world stopped because my grandma was the healthiest person I knew—she always took her vitamins and medicines on time. She never missed the doctor's appointment, so I really tried to understand how she had leukemia. She refused chemo, so we were told that she had months to live, and I tried to figure out how this was even life because the last thing I heard about cancer was my grandpa and that messed me up pretty bad.

It's almost Thanksgiving, so I was preparing my finances to go home and ended up taking the bus because it was cheaper than flying. I take the bus from Greensboro to Richmond, Richmond to New York, NY to Boston. I was told that Nana had been in and out of the hospital getting treatments, but as soon as I got to New York, I was told that while she was home, she was on an oxygen tank and to not freak out when I saw her. I was losing my mind on the inside while trying to remain calm. I didn't know why I wasn't told that when I was in Greensboro. The bus ride from New York to Boston did not allow ample time to process such things. Unfortunately for me, the bus was moving so slow that it was hours behind schedule. When I finally get to Boston, about four hours later than I was supposed to, I booked it to Nana's apartment with my suitcase. I was running from Back Bay station to Nana's house.

I get there and I see her, and she does, in fact, have an oxygen tank. I gave her a hug and a kiss, told her that I love her, and I missed her. I told her that I brought her nightgown with me (she left it after graduation), and I hang it up in her closet. I then go to the bathroom and break down. I never thought I would have to imagine a world without my Nana in it because like most Black families, she was the invincible pillar. We were just crumbling, and I didn't know what to do. I saw my mom cry, trying to process what was going on with her mother.

Thanksgiving was always my favorite holiday because I would get to see my Nana shine and help her with things. That wasn't happening this year. She stayed in bed most of the day, but she ended up being rushed to the hospital because she said she couldn't breathe. The EMT workers came, took her to the hospital and they told us flat out that if she went home again, she'd be right back, so leave her there.

I didn't understand why things were escalating so fast. They said we had months when, in actuality, we only had days. I remember being in the hospital room, looking at her and I watched her take her last breath. She was gone. It was right then and there that I had my first panic attack. I couldn't believe it. Now, I can't get that sight out of my head.

I knew she was proud of me, as she told me at my graduation. I just wish we had more time. I wish I could scratch her dandruff. Pay her Macy's card bill. Sit and watch stories (soap operas) and baseball with her. Those moments were gone and no matter how much I asked and prayed for them, I could never get them back.

One night I was sitting in my bare apartment, facing eviction, sad about my Nana and sad about existing. Losing her really put a void in my spirit. Now I was losing my apartment; no reason for her to be proud of me at all because I messed up way more than I didn't. I didn't have a man. I didn't have anything. I did have anxiety medicine and a couple of bottles of E&J. I put on my Sade CD, popped a couple pills, and drank.

And drank.

And drank.

And drank. I wanted to die. There was truly no reason for me to exist anymore. Yes, I had been blessed with life, but I was mismanaging it, and I didn't deserve it anymore. I wish I could have given it to my Nana because people loved her. They cared about her. They wanted her. Nobody wanted me. I sat there and drank some more. I knew that when I stopped, so would my heart and I was completely fine with that.

I heard a knock on my screen door. I was confused at first. I had zero tolerance for pop-ups. You're not just going to pop up at my apartment without calling first; I would leave you outside. On this particular day, I managed to get up and move the blinds and see that it was my line sister Sharlie. Surprisingly, I let her in. She said she just had a feeling to come by, so she did. She looked at me, concerned, and I just cried. God orchestrated her path that day. He also allowed me to live that day because I cannot tell you how I did. I just wanted to go to sleep and not wake up. I wasn't scared of hell. I just did not want to be alive anymore. I'm thankful for Him, and her, saving me that day.

I did end up getting evicted. The day I got access to the apartment to get the last of my stuff out, I actually ended up staying there for three additional days because I had nowhere to go. I threw away new things that I had, and I gave away what I could, but I had to wait for my flight back to Boston, so I stayed there in the cold for three days. Thankfully, no one came to the unit or I'm sure I would have been arrested. I vowed that I would never put myself in the position to be evicted again.

I got back to Boston, back to the house with my mom and just floated through life for a bit. I got my job back at City Sports and I even started working at the library again just to do something that didn't involve me really talking to anybody. I felt like a failure. Yes, I had my degree, but Boston no longer brought me joy. It was like a bad vacuum that kept sucking me in and I felt so unalive there.

I decided to create a plan and I would stay home for a year then I would move back to Greensboro. I hated Greensboro when I moved there, but there was something about being away from home and putting forth the effort in trying to survive that I had to go back to show myself that I could do it. I needed to prove to Nana that she was proud of me for something, and I could actually do it by myself, and I did just that when I moved back to Greensboro in 2008.

Part 3: Boomerang

When I got back in town, I stayed with my friend Patrice (not Boston Patrice) and focused on working. I was focused this time around; I needed to truly make Nana proud. I was able to secure a job at Macy's. Shortly thereafter, I got a job working in a call center for a credit card company, working in Collections. I went through training and excelled in the collector role very quickly, making monthly bonuses and exceeding goals. I moved up quickly to a job coach and assisted my peers in call monitoring and things like that. It was really good, and I felt very productive, like my life finally had meaning, that I was really doing something that was worthwhile and had purpose.

I was making money that I hadn't made before. Just as quickly as it got in my hands, it was going out of them. Having operated at a deficit for so long, finally having a surplus with no management skills was a recipe for disaster. Shopping was my vice. It was a great escape from my emotions. Yes, I did come back to Greensboro in order to prove that I could do more, and I was, but I wasn't satisfied with it, and it was driving me insane. I didn't think I ever properly processed the ending of any romantic relationships. When I attempted to think about them, I would drown my thoughts in liquor. I just wanted to be loved, and even money couldn't buy it for me.

Could these feelings be construed as "daddy issues"? Absolutely, because they were. My earthly father wanted nothing to do with me; my Spiritual Father wanted everything, but I was a mess and could not give it to Him. So, I was in these streets. Obviously, that trauma from that mirror lesson at church was no longer scary to me. Anyone who wanted me, I let him have me. I tried to be a hoe so bad, but I could see that that wasn't God's plan for me. My free will was running amok. Men I wasn't even attracted to were given the time of day. I forced myself into liking someone because he liked me, and I did that way more often than I'd like to say.

Falling apart on the inside, I was having the time of my life from the outside. My friends and I went to all of the Greek picnics and I'm talking everywhere: Atlanta, Florida, Texas, DC, Virginia. It was just a way to escape. Unfortunately, every guy that I dealt with, even the ones I forced myself to like, they didn't even want me long-term. They wanted me just enough to get the physical aspects of me and that was it; I fell for that every time. The guys that genuinely liked me, I brushed them off and sat them comfortably in the friend zone. Silly behavior, but it tracked.

One day I realized my job offered tuition reimbursement, so I decided to get a master's degree. It was reminiscent of my decision to initially move south and definitely resembled my decision to come back. I would do things differently than I did with undergrad. I also had a plan, because getting this advanced degree would help me solidify my ultimate goal of being in management. I had a plan, and it was time to execute.

Many times, I would think back to my youth, trying to piece together where I went wrong, and I continuously came to the same thing. I remember my cousin Niecy having a conversation with me and she would tell me, "Go back to your first love." Let me explain Who she was referring to.

Outside of her, my family wasn't a church-going family. There was a choice, and the majority chose not to go, unless it was a baby dedication or a funeral. Being in church for me was a welcomed escape. People could see me. They welcomed me with open arms and wanted to make sure I was comfortable. This wasn't something I experienced consistently. The mannerisms felt genuine, and I loved those feelings.

After the questionable experiences I had at my childhood church, I wanted to be certain that the church I attended in college was going to be the best fit for me. I was on a mission, visiting different churches with friends and trying to find one that would be "it." I remember one of my roommates and I would go to a specific church for midday Bible study just because they had free lunch. Shameful, but we were hungry college students.

I went to another church with one of my college friends and I specifically asked her if they ask first time guests to stand up. I hated that because I did not want to be singled out; I just wanted to go to church, experience the Word, and go about my business. She assured me that this church, considered a mega church, did not do that. Lo and behold, I go with her, and they ask for first time guests to stand. Reluctantly, I stood up. Just my luck that day I was the only first-time guest. A swarm of church members came up to me to hug me and greet me. I almost jumped out of my skin. I did not go back to that church for quite some time.

I did not want to live life being contained and afraid of my own voice. It was really hard to rest in the fact that maybe there was no right church for me. I made my commitment to God that I accepted Jesus and that I would be involved in His church, but I really didn't know how to approach it. I visited churches of all sizes and was having no luck finding the one for me. It was yielding the same results as my search for someone to love me intimately like I wanted.

I tried to maintain my relationship with God during the search. As much as I wanted to rest in God and seek Him, He was still a him, and men just did not have love for me. I definitely kept Him at a distance because I didn't understand me and if I didn't understand me, who, including God, really could? Since He wouldn't give me that man or any man to love, I chose not to give Him the time He deserved. I was finding my way, traveling through the wilderness like the hardheaded Israelites. I was thankful for His covering, but my trust issues halted my progress to my Promised Land. If I chased Him like I chased every "him" He created, it wouldn't have taken over a decade to find a great church home. Thankfully, even when I was thinking, "out of sight, out of mind" that God still had me in His sights and protected me, even from myself.

It had been years since I had talked to Leek, yet one day I decided that because he was a man who loved my body and who I thought loved my mind, I could speak with him about why nobody loved me. Perhaps he could tell me something that would trigger the light bulb in my brain to make me get it together. Now, I know you're wondering why would I talk to a man as opposed to talking to God? Because God never made me feel like he did, so it made sense.

At the time, I knew that he was engaged, and I made it

known out the gate that I was not interested in being disrespectful to his relationship, and that I just wanted to speak with him about me, and how I kept missing the mark with regard to love. He agreed to call me, and the conversation was very chill. It was very to the point, and he told me flat out that it was obvious that I didn't like me, which left opportunity for me to be misused. His exact phrase was "you gotta look at the common denominator and the common denominator is you." His words seemed harsh, but they weren't received as such. I could see that what he was saying was right. I knew that I had to implement changes or else I would be on this lonely hamster wheel for the rest of my life.

We caught up a little bit and I knew that he had another child, so I congratulated him on that and that was the conversation. There was no flirting. There was no conversation about the past. That was it. I got off the phone, went home, thought about what he said and tried to determine how I would get it together.

A couple of weeks had passed since that conversation. I was having a party at my house, which became my new thing (better to have parties and drink surrounded by people than be by myself) and I hit him up, letting him know that I was having a party and both he and his fiancée were invited. He replied that he was going to be unable to attend because he was moving, and I said, "Dang! House #2" and he replied, "No, apartment #1." I just said "okay" and that's when he let me know that he and his fiancée were breaking up. I told him I was sorry to hear that, to which he replied, "I'm not."

I replied "okay," and backed out of that conversation quickly.

After the party, he reached out to me, and it was from there that we started talking again. We really started off in a friendly way, as if we hadn't known each other for years. I kept my conversation short and tried to keep it very platonic, though it was very obvious that on his side he was looking for more than that. Based on the history we had, I was uninterested in jumping in with him because I knew how that had worked out for me in the past, and I wanted more than physical bonding. I started to see that I was worth everything that I wanted. I had been kicked and stepped on by a whole bunch of boneheads since the time that he and I dealt with each other, and I knew that wasn't something that I was going to put up with anymore. I had my guard up and things were playing out in a very refreshing, yet odd way.

By this time, we were also working at the same call center, with him working in customer service as a part-time sales associate. I was in management, so I had teams that I worked with; he would come up to my office and visit me and shoot the breeze. I'd stop by on my breaks and visit him downstairs. Again, very refreshing interactions.

We spent long nights on the phone talking, even when we would see each other at work the next day. One day, we were having a conversation and I let it be known that my favorite singer, Teedra Moses, was coming into town. He asked me if I was going to the show, and I told him I wasn't sure yet because I didn't know if I had to work. Days go by and on Thursday, he texts me asking what time he needed to pick me up. I'm confused because I did not recall any plans being made to link up because we hadn't done that yet. When I asked him what he was talking about, he texted me back saying, "Now you know I couldn't let your favorite singer come in town and you not be in the building."

I lost my mind. I screamed in my office, and everyone turned and looked at me like I was crazy. This man purchased tickets for us to see Teedra Moses at the Carolina Theater and I was baffled because again, we've known each other nine years at this point and he's never taken me anywhere, let alone on a date.

I was blushing and really happy about this date. That night, he picked me up with flowers in hand. We stopped by a bar downtown; I had a lemon drop martini. We went to the show, and it was amazing. He had never done anything like that for me before. He listened, he plotted, and he executed flawlessly. That was not the person that I knew when we were in college. He definitely earned all types of cool points that day, including a bonus prize.

We floated on what I considered to be a healthy bliss for a few more months. Then, on April 14th, 2012, while hanging out at my place, he decided to tell me how happy he was with me and how he had been enjoying our time together. He asked me if I wanted to be his girlfriend. I giggled, pretended to think about it, and I told him, of course the answer was yes. The past six months with him had been what I dreamed of. He was courting me. He was prioritizing me. He was seeing me outside of what my genitalia had to offer.

I was elated. We made it Facebook official and all of our friends lost their minds. You could say we broke the Internet that day with the announcement. I had previously met his children and before I knew it, we were moving in together. That was my idea and very premature, but we were spending all that time together anyway, it made sense that we stay together, so we did.

One thing I wanted to do in our relationship was to be as much of an upstanding, proper woman that I could be and, in this relationship, that meant speaking to the mothers of his children and getting an idea of if there were any issues held against me that needed to be addressed. I know that sounds crazy, but given the history between Leek and me, there was a bit of bad blood between me and both mothers of his children. One said she had no issues, and everything was cool; different story with Keisha. I asked her if we could meet at the mall to talk, and she agreed. When we met, I repeated why I wanted to sit down with her and asked if she needed anything cleared up. The response was very much her: she let me know that she was not worried about me being around her kid; in her own words, "I just don't like you, and nothing is going to change that." I respected it and that was that.

One thing about our rekindled relationship that made me happy was that this version of Leek went to church. One day during our courtship, he asked me if I would go with him to church. An intrigued me said yes, and that's when I was introduced to what would become my church home. As soon as I walked in, it felt like home. Everyone was genuinely welcoming and happy, like God was doing incredible things in their lives. That conversation I had with Niecy about "getting back to my first love" would play in my mind repeatedly, and I was glad to finally get back to that place. We would attend church every Sunday. Soon, I would join the housekeeping committee and I wanted to join the church immediately. We spoke about it, but I waited for his lead, as he said he wasn't feeling moved to join yet. We kept going, staying active in the ministry and about a year or so after my initial visit, he decided he was ready to join.

Crazy enough, after joining and getting back in with my first love, I finally had the desire to be water baptized. This is something that I ran from as a child. While I did get saved when I was younger, I remember feeling like getting dipped in that water would have me come up and there would be fire and brimstone. Why did I think that my baptism would cause such things to occur? I don't have an answer for that, but there were multiple times that, at my old church, I would say I was getting baptized, they printed my certificate, and I would not come to church that day or I just could not do it. It was amazing that 20 years later I finally decided to commit to my Savior and get water baptized.

I told Leek about it, and he was excited for me. I told a couple of my friends from church, and they were excited as well. They accompanied me that special day and I was water baptized. It just felt right to finally do it. (If you're reading this, you know that the world chose, in fact, not to end that day. Amen!) I felt really good to finally be reconnecting with God. Even more, our relationship was doing well. I knew that I was on the right path and that God was guiding me in what was happening.

I would like to say that the relationship between Leek and I just continued to get better. That would be false. There was always something that just was not right. There were endless requirements of me as a girlfriend. By requirements, I mean expectations of me being a wife without the ring, or caregiver without the paycheck. Whenever I would question something or not respond the way that he wanted me to, the only option was for him to choose to break up with me.

The first time this happened was because I chose to work overtime and would not cancel it to watch one of the kids. I don't know why he would not take off work, but he wanted me to, and I told him I would not miss the extra money. He was furious and said that I could have not worked overtime, and I could have watched the child, that my putting overtime above the family meant that I wasn't serious about him and if I wasn't going to care about his kids the way I cared about him, then I needed to leave.

I was so shocked at this point that I didn't know what to do with myself. I dropped to my knees and said, "please don't do this." Why was that my response? Why was I begging? I had no idea. I had risked everything to be with him and now he wanted not to be with me because of a decision that I thought was sensible. I mean, why wouldn't he take off work? It was crazy and from that point on, things were just super, super weird. It was as if the person who courted me and paid so much attention to me didn't exist anymore. It was as if all of that was done just to rope me in and now that I'm roped in, I'm just stuck.

I would be a liar if I said that our relationship totally went downhill after that initial almost breakup; I would be a bigger liar if I said it got Hulk strong. We didn't even really break up, but the thought of losing him, after having fought for so long to have him, I just couldn't bear the thought. I found myself walking on eggshells in my own house because I wanted him to be happy. I put my own happiness to the side rather quickly because I wanted him, and he wanted me, and I needed to do whatever was necessary in order to keep him. I would look stupid at this point if I lost him. Everyone looked at us and saw us as "couple goals" and I wasn't prepared to handle any more loss. So, I sucked it up and did whatever I had to do.

There were times that he would talk to me about his female coworkers from his other job, and I would always think that they were too friendly. I mean, we lived together and surely he was not doing anything crazy with me living in the same house as him. He regularly began staying out with his friends and I was out with mine, too—unless the kids were over. I usually would stay in the house with them, playing house. That was the trade off and I wanted to show him that I could do it and that we had a good family going on.

I caught a bug for baking and decided to open a bakery. Random, I know, but this was who I was. I would take desserts to work, and everyone loved them, so I figured I should get paid for my work. It was great because I loved making cakes and even more, the smiles my cakes put on faces.

One day, I was working on an order and one of my really good friends came by. She said she noticed that I looked like I had been crying. I told her that earlier, Leek told me that he could not see himself marrying me. Her response was, "Well, when are we packing your things up and getting out of here?" I said nothing. I just went back to baking whatever it was that I had to have done. It's crazy because I did not open my mouth. I never told him how his words affected me. I just never wanted him to know. I just sunk deeper and deeper into myself. Why would you want to be with somebody who says they will never marry you? What was the point?

Before I knew it, our year one anniversary had come and gone. Year two anniversary had come and gone. Typically, during an anniversary, there was a fight happening. I dreaded anniversaries and was so happy when they were over. Year three was different. We actually had a pretty decent time. We went on a trip and it was great. Things felt stable.

That summer, he told me that he wanted to go on a trip to Jordan Lake (we would go there often with the kids), but he wanted it to be just the two of us. The day we were supposed to go, he was rushing around the house trying to get everything together, very erratic and stressed out. I didn't understand because we had gone to the lake multiple times, and it wasn't like we were going swimming or anything. It again, it was just he and I, which meant less stress to me. We finally got on the road. He drove and I just sat there, awkwardly. Super weird tension.

We got to the lake, had our lunch and chilled. Out of nowhere, he says, "You want to go walk around?" I shook my head yes, whatever. I was trying to not be weird, but he was being weird so there was that. We got to this spot, and he said he needed to go to the bathroom. Gross, because nature. Per usual, I stood there and waited. He came back and we walked a bit more, then stopped and looked at the water. He was hugging me from behind and asked me if I was happy. I told him yes. I asked him if he was happy; he said yes. Then, he asked me how I would feel about being like this forever. Confused, I asked what he meant by that, turned around, and he got down on one knee and he pulled out a ring. Immediately, I was 100% full ugly crying face. I tried to understand what was happening. I was overjoyed, but confused, but excited, but shocked, but really, really happy and I could not stop crying. I could barely even breathe.

He said something about his knees starting to hurt. I broke out of my shock and shook my head yes. He got me a beautiful black diamond ring (I love black diamonds). He put it on my finger. It was a little big, but I didn't even care because he proposed! I thought he didn't want to marry me, but he did. That meant that I had been doing something right, right? I called my mom. She told me she already knew because he called and asked her permission the day before. I freaked and started crying again. I called my sister; she didn't answer the phone. She did call back, however, and I told her what just happened. Her response? A "congratulations" blander and drier than the Sahara. (I don't know why I called her anyway, but yeah.) We stayed a little bit longer before deciding to go back home.

He asked if I wanted to get dinner and I said that would be fine. He asked me where I wanted to go. I always wanted to eat hibachi, so I suggested that. He said he'd call and make the reservation. I sat on the couch staring at my finger like it needed surveillance. He came in the room and said they didn't have any open reservations, so we'd go to this new Mexican restaurant. I. DID. NOT. CARE. He could've gone to McDonald's, and I would have eaten that.

We got to the restaurant and while I headed toward the host stand, he started to pull me to the left. I looked and I saw it was a table of people. I see my friend, Bird, and before I could open my mouth, I realized I saw other familiar faces. Bird lived in Virginia, so this was a crazy coincidence. What in the world was going on?

Everyone said "hi" and we all hugged. I started crying again and we all laughed, confused as a unit. Well, he told everybody that I had been working really hard on my website, which was true, and that I finally finished it and he wanted to have a dinner to congratulate me for the hard work. He then told me that no one knew truly what happened, so I screamed, "Oh my God, we're engaged!" Everyone was shocked, but then erupted in congratulatory responses. (I called a few missing friends and that didn't turn out the way I thought it would, so I'll leave that at that. Let's just say: some people aren't happy when water waves.)

It was just a beautiful thing. The effort that he put into that initial date, I hadn't seen it in years. He did it for our engagement, so that must mean that he was serious and all the acting weird was him trying, working hard to get the money for the ring and do all this stuff. Maybe I was being too harsh on him. He did want to marry me, and this was great. This WAS great, right?

Being engaged changed things. I felt happier, I felt worthy, and I wanted to keep that feeling going forever. Unfortunately, that wasn't going to happen. A couple of months after we got engaged, Leek decided we needed more space, so we moved into a house. I thought this was a bit premature, considering he just signed a new lease with the apartment, but he broke the lease and we moved into a single-family home, right next door to his brother. The house was a mess, but he wouldn't listen to me about it, so I went with the flow.

The move put a major strain on our relationship because he didn't like to be challenged. There was so much tension that I sought counsel from one of the couples at church. They came by the house, and we discussed what our opportunities were, as well as what things needed to be fixed. There wasn't really a resolution because I could tell he was really upset that I even called this couple over to help us. That was not the result that I thought it was going to be, but there was no talk of breaking up or ending the engagement, which relieved me.

I had been feeling incredibly tired and insufficient and I didn't know what to do about it. I had gotten a severance from my job at the call center because they were going into a work at home environment, and we were not able to accommodate that in our apartment. I paid off his car and some of my personal debt, and thought that as a team, we'd be stable. I was feeling really lost. Leek was no solace for me. He said I needed to find another job quickly.

I couldn't understand why I was so emotional, so I decided to go to my doctor. I thought I had cancer or something because it was hereditary, and I was prepared for that diagnosis. I was talking to my nurse, and she asked me if there were any possibility that I could be pregnant. I said no. She asked if I had been engaging in the activity that could potentially get me pregnant and I said yes. As nicely as she could, she said, "Well, let's just take a test just to see."

I said, "Alright, if you want to waste a pregnancy test. Go for it."

We're sitting there and waiting for the results to come back and when the time was up, she got the results and showed it to me. I was pregnant. I was not prepared for that. I immediately started crying, trying to understand what I was going to do. I was a failure. I told her I was supposed to be getting married and she jokingly said, "Well, the baby will be here before the wedding" and I told her that wasn't funny.

Not even a second later, I began thinking about the close friends I had that struggled with fertility and how they had been doing everything to have children and they couldn't. I immediately started wailing and screamed, "God, please don't take my baby! I'm sorry!" The nurse told me to get it together and she called my doctor, who at the time was a male. He came in and said, "So, Reasha, what do you want to do?" I replied, "John, give me a minute! I'm trying to process the fact that I'm pregnant." He said, "well, you know, think about what you want to do and then let me know" and walked out the room. I calmed down, checked out and went to my car.

I called my friend Joseph as I was driving. He was excited; that was, until I burst into tears. He reassured me that things would be okay, but I did not think that at all. I went home and tried to deal with the news because who planned on being pregnant, not Reasha. I sat in the car thinking, "oh crap, I'm about to be baby mama #3". This was terrible. This was going to be bad, bad, bad,

bad, bad. Got home and he was there, surprisingly early. I tried not to panic. He asked me how my day was. I told him it was fine. He asked if I decided to go to the doctor. I told him I did. He said, "What did he say?" I hid behind the refrigerator, and I let him know that I was pregnant. He looked at me and he said, "well, how are you feeling?"

I said, "I'm scared."

He replied, "Why? It's okay." I started to cry and said, "Is it?" I went in the bedroom to go lay down on the bed and he said, "Everything's gonna be fine," kissing my forehead. I told him I wanted to take a nap. He replied, "I'll be right back" and left. My brain was losing itself at this point—I knew he was never coming back. He was going to move out of the state and we would never see each other again. I was preparing to be a single mother. In reality, he just wanted to go smoke.

Pregnancy and planning a wedding were not on my list of things to do but when you do the ACT, you're liable to get a really awesome gift out of it. That's what I got. We ended up changing wedding plans. I told my mom about the baby, and she was happy. I told my circle, who I think was happy. We had previously planned to go to Boston for my high school reunion, so that opportunity was used to let all my other family and friends know. They were really excited and yes, Baby Taylor was due to arrive May of the following year. Trying to plan a wedding was ghetto, so I opted to shrink things since I'd be getting married pregnant.

My pregnancy was amazingly easy—no morning sickness, few mood swings, and few cravings, but my patience had decided that at any given time, enough was enough and I was not going to be bothered. I was amazed that God allowed me the honor of carrying this blessing, because I never thought I would be a mother. I was super cautious about everything. I stopped running every morning for fear I would fall and hurt the baby; I barely used profanity, my dialect of choice since sixth grade. I was eating healthier, which I didn't even think was possible. Everything for my baby boy, who I named Almond Joy, because Almond Joys (boys) have nuts, Mounds (girls) don't. Corny, but it worked for me. We were operating as a team, waiting for his arrival. Leek would come with me to my doctor appointments, talk to the baby, cuddle with me, all the things a woman needed when she felt fat while pregnant.

I had gotten closer with his mom, Annette, during my pregnancy. She was the sweetest person. She had New Yorker all in her voice, yet it was surprisingly calming. Her smile would immediately put me at ease. When her son was acting a fool, she'd get him back in line. She really jumped in and was there for me emotionally since my mom was so far away.

January 2016, Annette and his dad, Leonard, came to stay with us for a few weeks. They parked their camper in the driveway and made sure to spend time with family. Annette was out and about, living her best life. She had a sleepover with her sisters and cousins, spent time with all of her grandkids, imparting peace and wisdom. It was really beautiful to see. One day after work, we sat in the camper, and she told me what my Almond Joy was going to look like. I was in awe and cried. I knew he was going to be beautiful, and I didn't know what connections she had to be able to tell me what he was going to look like, but I was here for it.

It was a Sunday when they decided to head back home, and I was devastated. I really enjoyed the time we were spending together, and I knew Leek loved having his parents around; their presence made him better. I was literally crying at the door, and Annette told me to relax and that she would be back on Thursday because she had an appointment that Leek was taking her to. She smiled that big, beautiful smile, and they went on their way. We went back to business as usual, had dinner and settled down to watch "The Walking Dead."

Tuesday night, we were in bed, and I tried to find a comfortable position for my belly. Leek could not sleep. He tossed and turned and also could not get comfortable. I asked him if there was something on his mind, and he just reiterated that he couldn't sleep. I tried rubbing his back, didn't work. We prayed for peace over his mind, didn't work. This went on for hours. When he was finally able to be still, his phone rang. He answered, and it was Leonard. He sat up abruptly then said, "What? I'm on my way." I asked him what was going on, and he was frozen. He looked at me and said, "Pops said my mom is dead."

That was not a call any of us were expecting. I quickly hopped up and got dressed. He was moving in slow motion for obvious reasons. He told me that I didn't need to go with him, but I was going, and I was going to drive. We immediately headed out. It was the quietest ride we ever had. He was trying to process what was going on, calling his aunt and siblings. Leonard lets him know that the EMS workers were on the way.

We finally got there, and I'll spare the details of what we saw. Just know it was a horrible sight that is probably burned into everyone's brain. Heading back, he was trying to be strong. I held his hand, letting him know that whatever he was feeling was valid and that I was there for him. I distinctly remember him saying that he remembered that his mother told him that she was proud of him. He started to cry, but just as quickly as he started to cry, he stopped. It was like he had to reel himself in, that he couldn't show that emotion. For religious reasons, Annette was cremated. The family pulled together resources so that she could have a really nice service.

The death of my [almost] mother-in-law was a pivotal point in our relationship for obvious reasons. Having never lost a parent, I could not relate to him the way he needed. I asked my mom to reach out to him because she had experienced the same when Nana passed away. That was a bonding moment for the two of them and I appreciated my mom for that because again, I had nothing to offer in that situation, unfortunately.

Navigating grief is such a challenge, and there isn't one set way of processing it. I tried to allow him space to deal with what happened while simultaneously trying to get the wedding together and waddling around pregnant. When he lashed out at me, I didn't take it personally because I knew that he was going through something to which I could not relate. I told him it would be a good idea to go to therapy, seek counseling for grief or talk to our pastors. I suggested anything and everything that could get him to deal with his emotions, and he would always refuse. All I could do was pray and just love him through it.

On April 15th, we got married. It wasn't the wedding of my

dreams— my brothers and majority of my blood relatives were absent. My sister was also absent and given the way she responded when I called her about the engagement, I was not expecting to see her anyway. Lots of people important to me were missing, yet a good amount was there. I was marrying the man I thought was the man of my dreams, so it made everything okay. I was very pregnant, so there was no participating in libations. I safely danced around and laughed with my friends. It was an exciting time. We did a tribute to Annette, of course. Leek did what he did, which was get super drunk with his friends and have a ball.

We went home, prayed with the kids then slept, because we had consummated enough prior to our wedding night. We woke up, had a quaint baby shower, and then began trying to settle into married life.

Part 4: Married Life Strife

Three weeks after the wedding, my first born, my Tristan was born. I was supposed to get my hair done that day, but my sweet boy had things to do, like coming into this world. Because I was super scared of having an epidural, I had my child naturally. Husband was right there, holding my hand, telling me I was doing a fantastic job, just being supportive. It was everything, unlike the doctor who was supposed to be delivering my child, but that's a story for a different day.

When my son was placed on my chest, my world just shifted in the best way ever. It was so beautiful, and he was going to be the recipient of every bit of love that I could muster. I was proud to be his mother, proud to be Husband's wife, just proud that God was showing favor to me with all of the things in my life. I could not have asked for more at that time.

Having a newborn is all fun and games until that newborn does newborn things. I was sleep deprived. My breasts were in pain from nursing, and I was a walking mess. All I knew was Tristan was having trouble latching and I didn't want to give him formula. When I finally broke down and had to give my baby formula, I felt like a failure again, and all of those old emotions came right back to the surface. I supplemented until we were able to get him to latch perfectly, and I hated doing that.

Husband began to pull away and I didn't have his help because he was unavailable emotionally. I was a bit surprised that I did not get any assistance from him, considering this was my first but his third child. He was very hands off with the baby, and I had a tough time dealing with that. I was the new parent here, so I thought that I would get way more, which was frustrating. I then reminded myself that he was going through grief, so I let a lot slide.

As months passed, he refused to do anything to be better. He was smoking more. He was drinking more. He was away from our family more; the only time he would be around us was when it was time to go to church on Sunday. I took what I could get and tried to manage my emotions. I later realized that I had postpartum depression, but I didn't know how to go about getting any type of assistance with processing that.

Waiting On My Rainbow

One specific day, I was home trying to nurse our son. I was sitting in the bedroom, and he came in demanding that I move my car. Apparently, I had blocked him in, and he was pissed about it. I pointed out that I was nursing, which he could clearly see, and told him it would be a few minutes, but he could get my keys and move it if he wanted. He started yelling at me, telling me to move it immediately and being really ignorant. I not so nicely told him to watch his mouth and watch who he was talking to, ending by telling him to wait until I finished nursing. He stormed out the room, slamming the door. I thought nothing of it.

I finished nursing the baby, put him down for a nap and went outside. His car was gone and so was mine. Baffled, I walked down the driveway and looked in the cul-de-sac to see he drove my car straight into the cul-de-sac and left it there, the doors wide open. It was raining at the time. I was livid because why would he do that? I got my keys off the driver's seat and put my car back in the driveway.

I didn't say anything about it. This was bad even for him and I was starting to think grief had nothing to do with it. I kept trying to seek counsel from people at church, but it wasn't really working. I leaned into praying more, asking God to show me why things were what they were. Surely my heavenly love could help me fix my earthly love.

Unfortunately, I was let go from my job because I kept taking time off to handle the baby. When I told Husband, he was furious. This was another thing for him to despise me for. It got to a point where I felt like marriage wasn't the thing for us because we were not gelling like we were supposed to. He wasn't letting me in. I wasn't letting him in, and I didn't know what to do. I was talking to my mom, and she told me to come home, so I packed a bag for me and the baby and I went home to Boston. It was Thanksgiving, and I figured being away from him for a week would give him time to get it together. It would give me time to clear my mind and I'd be able to come back, and things would be fine. I left a message on the refrigerator, letting him know we were leaving. He didn't call me or say anything.

I would call him every day while I was there, and he

wouldn't answer my calls. I would text him that I loved him. He wouldn't reply. I happen to go on Facebook on Thanksgiving Day, and he put a video up telling everyone to enjoy their time with their family. I noticed his wedding ring wasn't on. That upset me. I sent a message to his aunt because I knew he was at her house, and she said his wedding ring was on and everything would be fine.

When I got back, we talked, and I could feel a shift and that things were not going to be the same. He used words like abandonment and parental kidnapping with regard to me taking Tristan with me, and I looked at him like he was crazy, as well as tried to figure out who it was he was talking to because this was not verbiage he would normally use. We met with our pastors. They told me that I was wrong for leaving and we should have talked about it as husband and wife. I accepted responsibility for that and tried to get us back on track. Truly, there was no track, and I would quickly realize that sooner than I thought.

As that year ended and the New Year began, we did try to be better as a unit and it was really spotty, but we were doing it. I got rehired at my prior job, so I was working again. It's crazy to think that you're going into your one-year wedding anniversary while still processing the gravity of the mistake that you made. We went to Myrtle Beach and that was a trip, indeed. We forced ourselves to have fun. Even in the tension, there was still love in there, hanging on for dear life.

Tristan would be turning one soon and I was joyfully planning his birthday party. A random day at work, my friend Renee walked by me as she was going to clock in for the day. She quickly doubled back to me and said, "Oh my God. You just looked super pregnant." I was so furious I snapped at her, saying, "How dare you! You know I'm trying to finish a year of nursing Tristan so I can get my body back! Why would you say something like that?" She apologized, saying she "just saw it." Hmph!

When I got home, I told Husband what she said, and he suggested I take a pregnancy test. (After one child, having pregnancy tests on standby is just a part of basic standard operating procedure.) I went to take the pregnancy test because I just knew I

Waiting On My Rainbow

was not pregnant. I could count on one hand the number of times that we engaged in intercourse in the past year, so being pregnant would be insane.

Immediately upon urinating on the stick, pregnant. I took four tests and got the same result. I knew exactly the date of conception, considering sex was infrequent and wasn't a pleasurable experience anymore. I was mad. He didn't provide a response of concern. The next day, I called my doctor, who dismissed me, saying it was too soon to be tested by them because I wasn't even six weeks. I had to wait, so I scheduled the appointment. I went to work and just shook my head at Renee. Welp, baby Taylor #4 was now on the way.

I would ask God to show me what I was supposed to be doing and what I could do to fix things. Tristan had turned one, summer was approaching, and I felt nothing but emptiness and solitude. My second pregnancy was the total opposite of my first. I had horrible morning sickness; I could not get comfortable. I just knew that this baby was going to be a girl. I exhaled deeply when I found out this baby would also be a boy. Husband paid no attention to me, whether I was fat and pregnant or not, and I thought that God forgot about me, too. I didn't know what to do, outside of make sure these two boys had the best life possible.

December rolled around and I went into labor five days early. I was cognizant of what was happening because, you know, it wasn't my first rodeo. My friend Bird just happened to be in town and she and her friend Sarah took me to the hospital. They notified Husband, who took exceptionally long to get there. I frantically wondered why, but a lot was happening. This birthing experience was terrible. I was yelled at by nurses. My water was broken for no reason. I was told that my child's umbilical cord was around his neck. All of the horrible things were happening, and I really felt like I was going to die, as was my son.

Husband finally got there, and he looked... annoyed. He was not being the supportive coach he was with Tristan just a year ago. I needed calm and I got it from Bird. Go figure. After what felt like an eternity, they got my son out safely. He was placed on my chest and as I looked at him, I felt a forearm in my uterus.

106

Long story short, I would not stop bleeding after they got Dylan out and they had to pull out blood clots. The whole room looked horrified yet was really quiet; I just felt cold and like going to sleep, but they were telling me not to. They ended up getting the bleeding under control and Husband lashed out, telling me that we weren't having any more children. He specifically said, "I'm not going to lose my wife for children, so this is it." I agreed because I didn't want to die either, so, fine, Husband, whatever you say.

I spent the night in the hospital with Dylan alone. It ended up being two nights because they had to schedule his circumcision. I had arranged for Jenny to watch Tristan, but Husband insisted on going home to "handle" things. I assumed that meant smoking, which I had no chance of winning against. The next morning, he brought Tristan with him, so he got to see his little brother and I got to see my baby. Seeing my two boys made me so happy and fulfilled. Things were weird, but I had two incredibly good reasons to push through my unconscious thoughts of self-sabotage. My family was going to be fine.

We got home after the circumcision and I was, at the least, confused about life trying to juggle two little people. Days after getting home, Christmas Eve to be exact, Husband decided to have a party in the garage. I did not think this was a good idea. I actually thought this was a terrible idea because I literally gave birth days ago, and I voiced this to him. He didn't care and invited people over anyway.

I sat in the house with the babies and tried to understand what was happening. I didn't want to be rude, so I got up, slowly, and went in the garage and talked to everyone. Just as quickly as I went in, I went back in the house because I felt out of place, in my own garage. It had been well over a year since his mom passed. It was coming up on two years and things were not better and I couldn't figure out why. I had resorted to saying nothing because if I said anything, it would lead to an argument, and I did not want to deal with that. My eyes and breasts couldn't be leaking at the same time.

I realized I was in survival mode. I had two children. I don't want to be a single mother, so I had to shut up and let him do whatever he did and keep praying over him that he was going to be better and that God was going to change his heart and that we could get to our happy place because at this point, I didn't even know what happy was outside of these children.

Our marriage really began to crumble after Dylan arrived. It was as if the compounded grief of losing his mother combined with my inability to navigate birthing two children and parenting two other children. Our marriage at that point was just for show. There were multiple times where he just did not want to be near me or want to touch me. I internalized everything. I did lose myself a bit, not dressing like I used to or trying to be sexy; I sucked at juggling Wife Reasha with Mom Reasha with Reasha Reasha. I didn't even go out with my friends anymore; I used the boys as an excuse to seclude myself.

Husband started working really late and I would regularly comment about his hours and how they weren't conducive to our family's success. He stated that he had to work those hours and that I just had to deal with it. That never really sat well with me because I didn't understand how someone who was a trainer at a call center would be at work till 11:00PM or midnight and later, but as was my custom, I just allowed the behavior.

I wasn't happy. I was trying to get back in with God and see what He had in store for me. I would ask Him to show me where I needed to be and, being the God that He is, He would show me things; I would think that God was drunk. There was no way that this marriage wasn't going to work because God let me marry him, didn't He? It's so funny how we act like free will is not a thing, like we can't just get up and do what we want. God gave us dominion over this earth, and we will act a fool with it and then blame it on either God or Satan, when both are somewhere minding their business and it is just our free will. (Believers, some of us are crazy.)

There were times in my marriage when I felt like I was living a horrible nightmare. It was like no matter how much I tried to please him nothing was sufficient. I had nothing left in me, yet I tried ridiculously hard to pour from that empty cup. Making him happy and giving the appearance of happy was my job; if I wasn't going to work, I wasn't going to leave the house. I stopped couponing, stopped anything that would have me interact with anyone because it was too much to be asked, "How are you?" and not be able to tell the truth. It was best to just stay home on those days and nights and just allow him to do whatever he was going to do. It wasn't like I could've kept him from it anyway.

One of the most degrading things that I allowed to happen was sex. There was a point in time when I couldn't keep my hands off that man. I wanted to do everything to be beautiful for him— keep my hair done, keep my body waxed, all of that. It was for HIM not me, but I was glad to do it because he would make me feel like the only woman in the world.

Until he didn't.

Sex became in unwelcome chore. Let's be clear: I know the "wife rule" and never denied my husband my body. (It was our body, after all.) Even when I was exhausted from nursing our kids, making dinners, and packing lunches, cleaning house, working 8-10 hours a day, I was available to him. Most days, I wanted the touch even though I knew it was an afterthought to him. I just wanted him to want something I possessed, even if it were just my body. I knew subconsciously there was something, some thingS going on, but I still just wanted to be wanted. Sex changed so drastically; because of all the distractions of life, I couldn't pinpoint if it was subtle or immediate. It got to a point where I didn't even get aroused. I dishonestly presented orgasms. I moaned when I wanted to cry. I knew he knew but he didn't care. The release was all that mattered to him, a selfish itch that needed to be scratched. It got so uncomfortable for me when there was no eye contact. He would just flip me over, fitting because I felt just like a dirty, worthless harlot when it was over.

I would continue to ask God to show me where I was supposed to be. He would show me something and I would ask him again because I didn't like what I saw. I refused to see my life without him in it. Again, I had no desire to be a single mother. I felt like that would be the self-fulfilling prophecy that I had sworn to avoid. Let's not ignore the whispers, the looks that would come because the "couple goals" couple ended in divorce. I did not want any part of it, so I just existed, and what a horribly lonely and sad existence it was.

Arguments were daily: about the bonus children, about work, about how I looked. He was so disgusted by me not dressing up and putting on makeup, forgetting the fact that we had a one-year-old and a newborn that I was trying to take care of with no assistance. I would repeatedly ask for help and it would go on deaf ears. I decided again to seek help from our church. One particular bogus conversation with a couple happened and by the end of it, this man had convinced Husband that I was bipolar, had a chemical imbalance, and needed help. I sat there in awe.

This man, at this particular time, had accepted boxer briefs from someone he claimed worked with him. I came home and they were opened, on OUR bed, for me to see like nothing was wrong. Everyone was ignoring that fact and telling me that I was bipolar. What man in his right mind would bring home underwear he didn't purchase himself and think his wife was not going to question that?

I felt like my back was against the wall and I was cornered, and I did not know how to fight my way out of it. I did what I've done one thousand times before, which was I just let it happen. There was no formal counseling that he would do. I thought about going myself, but the last time I did that I was prescribed so many meds I could barely remember my own name. I wanted to be a mom who was going to be the most emotionally sound and supportive for our four children. I was at a loss on how to get there. My free will had me bound.

While my marriage was a dumpster fire heading into our third marital anniversary, there was marital joy coming for someone close to me. My brother had proposed to his longtime love, and they were getting married. I was so excited for him. He had heard much of what was going on in my marriage and he offered the best advice that a brother could, which was appreciated. That's the type of person my brother was. Always able to see every side and give a non-biased opinion that is for the good of all parties involved, and that's one of many things I love about him.

They were getting married in April, the same week of our anniversary. This particular year was Husband's year to plan our anniversary and he wanted to go on a cruise. I thought it would be ridiculous to miss my brother's wedding, so, for once, I opened my mouth, and I told him that I would like to go to the wedding. He was totally against that idea, saying that we had gone to Vegas before and he didn't want to go again. I wasn't so much concerned with the fact that it was Vegas as much as the fact that it was my brother's wedding. He said no and was firm with that no. Against my better judgment I sided with Husband.

As the time got closer to our anniversary, there were no plans. There had been no cruise conversation. There had been nothing done, and I asked what was going on so that I could plan accordingly for the kids and things of that nature. He lashed out at me, telling me that I didn't allow him to do anything, that he didn't want to go anymore because I was being difficult, and it was pissing him off. I was confused because I wasn't pushing the issue; I just said what I wanted to do, and he was against it. I allowed him the space and the opportunity to plan the cruise that he wanted to go on. He didn't follow through for reasons unknown to me. It would be a lie to say I didn't see that coming.

The week of our anniversary, he wasn't talking to me. I wasn't really talking to him, and I was at a crossroads on whether or not I was going to be able to be there for my brother's biggest day. I talked to my mom, and she told me that I needed to be there for my brother. I bought a ticket for myself to go to the wedding. I was just going to tell him that I was going. He could manage the kids while I was gone. Less than 24 hours later, I realized that I had made a mistake; I agreed to be one with this man and that we would be together even when we didn't agree. I didn't want to relive that Thanksgiving trip and its aftermath. After all of that, I didn't go to the wedding. I don't have many regrets in my life, but missing my brother's wedding is definitely one of them.

We didn't even talk on our anniversary. I don't even remember if he was home. There was no dinner. There were no flowers. There was no candy. There was no happiness. There was the nothing that I had become accustomed to. It was depressing. My old friends, Inadequacy and Self-Hatred, came back, reminding me that I was deserving of this because I was obviously a bad person and love was just not something that was sustainable in a romantic sense for me.

As always, I had to suck it up, deal with the kids and settle into the fact that this was going to be my life until the day that God called me home. I had again gotten into the space where I didn't want to bother God with my foolishness because he told me numerous times before how I could change things and I just did not want to do that. Complacency became my best friend. It was a miserable existence, but it was all I had.

With all the changes going on and all the financial issues we were having, I applied for a new job at another call center and was hired. While I would be working closer to our home, I did my training in a building that was next door to where Husband worked. One day, I was driving by, and I noticed that he was at his car speaking with a young lady. I decided to go say "hi" because why would I not?

I pulled into the parking lot in my minivan, Big Blue, let my window down, and waited to be acknowledged. For some unknown reason, I didn't get out the car. I noticed that when he noticed me, his face changed, and it looked like the conversation with the young lady changed. I was thinking this was one of his trainees, that he was just letting off some steam about work. Then, I noticed that they were arguing. I still didn't get out of the car. At one point in the conversation, he said, "well, there's my wife. Tell her." She looked at me, turned pale as a ghost, and walked off swiftly. Magically, I was finally able to get out the car.

I went to him, and I asked him what was going on and he told me that this young lady had been stalking him. Immediately, with my mouth not even moving to respond, he started screaming about how he didn't have time to cheat as well as some other things I zoned out on once I heard the word "cheat". I just looked at him, trying to make sense of what just happened in front of my goofy face.

I said, "Well, if you're not cheating, why are you upset?" I looked around the parking lot. The girl was nowhere to be found. I then said, "Well, hey, since you're off work early, can you go pick up the boys so I can go get things for dinner?" His response, a quick yes, let me know that something was wrong because he never wanted to handle the children himself. He went, got the kids. I got the items I needed for dinner, went home and cooked. There was no additional conversation about that parking lot incident.

A couple of weeks went by and again, we were just existing. We were more like roommates than spouses. Anything was cause for argument. Anything would set him off, so I tried not to talk. I tried to keep the kids quiet. I could've tried talking to him, could've been more concerned, but I didn't want to be called a nag. I did not want that ticking time bomb to explode.

One day, we were outside while the boys played, and I asked him if he wanted to come with me to get clothes for the boys. He said yes, but his demeanor said he really didn't want to, and I didn't know why he agreed because he didn't have to. I strapped both kids in the van and I finally asked him what was going on with him. He started shouting at me. I demanded that he stop yelling at me in front of the kids because I never wanted the children to see us argue.

He kept going, and now, I'm mad and I go off, too. I told him that he was acting like a baby daddy or something. He told me that I was acting like a baby mama, and he ripped me a new one. He took a breath and said to me, so easily that it rolled off his tongue with no hesitation, "you're a cancer in my life and I can't wait to get rid of you." A *cancer*. My husband told me that I was a cancer in his life, and he couldn't wait to get rid of me.

I immediately stopped talking. In my brain, I kicked him out the van and drove straight to Boston to my family, my safe place. In reality, I drove to Friendly Shopping Center, straight to Carter's, and got my babies the clothes they needed. My heart was beating so fast, yet I had to be calm. We got home, he went in the garage to smoke; I took care of the boys' dinner and nighttime routine and went to bed myself.

I was at a standstill. I couldn't think of anything worse than being called a cancer by the man that I loved and that I was married to. My Nana and Grandpa, my pillars, both died of cancer. Why would he say something so cruel? I texted him and said that we needed to truly go to counseling to get past whatever we were on, or we needed to separate. He replied that he wanted to separate.

I was crushed. He left that following weekend on Saturday without saying anything. The show must go on though, right? Monday, I got up. I made sure the kids were ready to go to daycare. He was supposed to come and get them, but I knew he was not dependable. He got there when he got there. I rushed away to work. The entire day at work I was tired. This was all my fault because I stayed quiet too long. There was no need to talk to God because this wasn't His doing; it was mine.

It was Monday, July 8th. I was physically present at work, but mentally I was somewhere far, far away. My coworkers were noticing that I was behaving different, and I vaguely let them know that there were things going on at home. I was just trying to be quiet and figure out what the next move for my family was going to be. He was still not coming home because he was wherever he was, so I was doing what I always did— everything, alone.

After giving the boys dinner, I decided to scroll on Instagram. I paused when I noticed that I had a follow request. I'm confused because the page was a kids' dance page. I wasn't sure why this page had requested to follow me because I had no daughters. As with any account that would send a follow request to my private page, I sent a DM asking if I knew the person. I got the reply of "I don't think so." I politely responded, "Well, you added me, so I'm just asking."

The next reply I get was something to the effect of, "Well, maybe you should reach out to our owner, Faith. Maybe your husband referred you to us." Suddenly, all the lights in the house came on and I realized what this was. This was the girl he was arguing with at work, the alleged stalker. Because I wasn't in the mood for foolishness, I replied back advising her that I had yet to have time for her little stalker shenanigans. I thought that was gonna be the end of it, because as I recalled, from what he was saying, it was nothing.

She replied, *No need for name calling. That's why your marriage is falling apart and I've been sleeping with your husband.*

I was immediately speechless, which for me was rare. I told her go to hell and she proceeded to tell me that she had been sleeping with my husband the majority of our marriage, beginning in fall 2017. She told me that she knew the hotel that he was staying at, that we both were horrible people, both verbally abusive, and that we deserved each other. I was in shock and that would be the only thing that could describe the crashing down of my life that happened so quickly in this Instagram exchange. This girl (term used loosely) proceeded to tell me my whole life story, that she'd been wanting to tell me about what was going on since I was pregnant with our second son, that she tried to tell me before what was going on, but I didn't respond. It wasn't actually until that moment that I found out there was a secret inbox on Instagram. Sure enough, when I scrolled through those messages that I consider spam, there was a message from December 2017 saying, "Leek cheats on you".

She knew everything. She told me that she knew that a famous rapper was my cousin and told me who that person was, which was just insanity because very few people even knew that about me, as I had never met him personally; I knew his mom, but it made zero sense as something he would talk to her about. I really didn't understand the purpose of that, but that's beside the point.

She proceeded to send me screenshots that she'd been saving since 2017. I read them, seeing how my husband was talking about how gross of a wife I was, how I was working overtime and how convenient that was because he had to stay home with the kids and how he was sad he couldn't see her. I started wailing, clutching my sink so I didn't fall, because my whole body was weak. Almost instantly, Tristan called for me. He got out his highchair and came to the kitchen. I turned my face away quickly because I didn't want my child to see me bawling like a baby. I didn't want him to see this hurt. I quietly told him to get back in his seat and I'd be right there.

I tended to the boys and went back in the kitchen. Now, did I have a feeling? Did my intuition tell me that there was something going on? Of course, the answer was yes. Did I want to believe it was as deep as it was? Of course not. I had been asking God to show me what was, and I had been ignoring the subtle signs, so an explosion was what I would get. No way to deny or ignore that.

I called the hotel where she told me he was; the hotel confirmed he was there. I attempted to get as much information from this girl as she was sending it. I racked my brain trying to figure out when did he have the time to do this, but as we all know, people make time for things they want to make time for. Unfortunately for me, as a wife, someone I thought was his best friend, as a mother of two of his children, the person who he took vows to love and protect and cherish, in sickness and in health, good times and bad, for better for worse, it was more important to satisfy whatever carnal desires he had with this random than with me.

I knew something was amiss. I allowed him to make me think that I was crazy, because why would he cheat on me? We had so many conversations about infidelity, and I always told him that I would rather he leave me than to cheat on me, as I could recover from the heartbreak of abandonment. I could not recover from being cheated on. She went so far as to tell me that she had sex with him in front of our house while the boys and I were sleeping. Bold.

I asked her if he ever bought her anything or if he ever took her out. She responded that they had gone to a few bars together, but he had not bought her anything, just some candy from a gas station. As soon as she said that my attitude changed. I said to her, "I pray that you learn your worth because you are a child of God and you're worth more than being some married man's side piece, aiding in destroying families over some Skittles." I immediately felt bad for her; worse for her than I felt for myself. I told her she could come collect him and his things and she declined, saying he was "one of many in rotation." I disagreed because who would keep text messages that span that length of time? Who would go through the trouble of stalking someone's wife? He hurt her somehow, so she chose to hurt him by hurting me.

I tried to figure out why this happened to me. What did I do to deserve this? I was going through all the stages of grief. Comically enough, she had the audacity to ask me to keep this off social media because she had a business. Lady [of the night], you told me that you'd been having an affair with my husband for two years; you're presenting said affair to me in the most negative, disrespectful way and had the unmitigated gall to ask me to respect your business? I politely told her that she could go to hell. Again, I told her she needed to learn her worth.

I read text messages where he was telling her that once we got married that I stopped doing all the things that got him to marry me. I didn't see how he forgot or chose to ignore the fact that I had children 20 months apart and had postpartum, but that was irrelevant to the fact that my husband wanted to get his physically desires handled regularly. To find out that my husband was out here doing husbandly things with whores that were in his training class at work, I was mortified.

I felt like I was drifting outside of my body and there was nothing that I could do. I finally stopped talking to her, and I cried my eyes out. I called my best friend and let her know what happened. I called my "break in case of emergency" crew and let them know what was going on. I didn't know what to do. I did not call my mother for obvious reasons. I was already at the Earth's core and couldn't bear getting any lower. If I could, I didn't want her helping with that.

Jenny ended up coming over. She gave me a hug and I cried, as crying was now the only language I could fluently speak. She wanted me to go to the hotel and beat the crap out of Leek, while she stayed at our house and watched the boys. I couldn't muster the energy. Jenny was persistent trying to get me to go over there but I didn't want to. Number 1: I wasn't ready. Number 2: I knew how I got when I got angry (read: black out), and I didn't want to end up on "Snapped" or "First 48", because who would take care of my children? Being the amazing friend she is, she prayed with me. I cried some more. She ended up going home and that night, I ended up having the boys come sleep in the room with me. I locked the bedroom door just in case he tried to come in, because by this point, I was quite sure that she told him, and that was that. I was unexpectedly force fed the blue pill. So, what's next?

I had to go to work the next day and put on a face. I didn't know whose face it was, but it wasn't mine. I made it through that day, and the next, and the next. Husband was M.I.A. and I was fine with that. That same week, I was running late for work and just threw something on. It was not workplace appropriate, but I did not want to be late, so I went with it.

There was this one supervisor who decided that would be the day she'd flex her authority and tell me to cover up. She told me and I did it, no problem. Lunch came around and I was off company time so I could do what I wanted, which was take the covering off. I came back from lunch, and she told me that I had to go home because I was out of dress code. I reminded her that lunch was not included in company time, and we got into a debate about it.

She took me into an office with my supervisor and tried to write me up and I lost it. I said, "you are getting upset with me over spaghetti straps meanwhile I just found out my husband is cheating on me! I don't give a flip about what you're talking about! Please let me just cover up and go back to my desk!" My supervisor turned beet red. I just walked out and went to my seat. I realized what I had done and began to shake. I did not need to get fired in addition to getting cheated on.

Neither of them followed after me. No one said a thing. My coworker saw me and tried to comfort me, telling me to breathe. The day ended and I left. Thank God I had that covering because I could have gotten fired. I probably should have, because that was still insubordination, but obviously they saw I was under a lot of stress.

I got home, saw no signs of him. I knew he still hadn't come home, so I texted him. He didn't respond. I didn't know what was going on in his brain. I barely even knew what was going on in mine. What I did know was there was a gun under our mattress and I was unaware of his frame of mind whenever he decided to come home. That being said, I hid his gun. Had he ever been physically abusive toward me? No, but with the emotional abuse and the financial abuse that we had been dealing with, on top of the infidelity, I was not going to leave anything open.

He finally came home, and he slept on the couch. No words or anything. It was all a blur. A very terrible blur. I could not run; I needed to face this once and for all. I let him know that we needed to talk about what happened. It was ridiculous that I even let him come back in the house; what was even more ridiculous was that he came back in the house and didn't think that he needed to immediately address what happened.

I decided to write down a list of questions that I want to ask because I wanted answers. I needed answers. I deserved answers. Looking back, I realized that nothing was going to make me feel at ease after finding out he had been unfaithful. There was nothing that could satisfy that.

On schedule, I internalized all of it, because it had to be my fault— I was dealing with the kids, not dressing like I used to, not behaving like I used to; these were all valid reasons, right? Everything was Reasha's fault because that was what he taught me to think, so that was what I operated in. Nevertheless, I was going to ask these questions because I needed to know answers.

We finally had our sit down and it was so pointless that I would have rather consumed a V8. He answered the questions vaguely. When I asked specific questions that warranted an open-ended response, he only repeated back, "I made a bad choice." I asked him why he came back home. He finally looked at me and said, "I just came home because I ran out of money." He wasn't remorseful. There were no tears. He apologized for what happened because he made "a bad choice." I looked at this person like who are you, and what happened to the man that I married, because he didn't live in this fleshly body anymore.

I didn't leave the conversation satisfied, so I called our pastors. We went to have a session with them, and I didn't feel better after that. They told me from a Godly perspective I had license to leave but, if I were to stay, I had to operate in forgiveness. In that, it meant that I couldn't withhold myself from him. I asked him to change his number; he was not willing to do that. Why were we even there? I had a lot of thinking to do.

We got home and held each other, and I cried some more. Did I have sex with him? Of course I did, because I really wanted to act like this whole thing didn't happen, that it was just a really, really bad nightmare. I just wanted my happy place back. Divorce is not a word you casually throw around in a marriage; when you use it, you better be sure that you know what you are doing. I learned that in the midst of this situation.

I forgave him, and that was the worst thing I could have done. From that moment on, he was worse. It was like he didn't want my forgiveness. He even said to me that he was glad that it all came out because he was tired of living a double life and he was tired of lying, which boggled my mind because the best way to not be tired of lying or living a double life was to, you know, LITERALLY NOT DO THOSE THINGS. I guess that piece of common sense wasn't common.

He changed. There was nothing better about the behavior. It seemed like he resented me and that was his out. I chose to forgive him and work on the marriage. I would not be able to forget, but I would work on building a bridge over this. Husband's actions showed that was not what he wanted. However, he failed to communicate that. This was that "worst" part of the marriage vows. For me, this was also that "sickness" part because I was literally sick to my stomach every day thinking about what happened.

While he refused to change his number, he said that I could have access to his phone whenever I wanted. He would take his password off and I could look at whatever would ease my mind. Any questions I had, he would answer, and I thought that was a step in the right direction. What occurred each time I asked to check or look at his phone? Attitude. Anything I asked him to do that he said he would agree to? Attitude. I talked to married people who dealt with infidelity and asked them how they got past it. I was really focused on rebuilding and minimizing any repeat offenses. I wanted the marriage to work.

One night, we were watching a movie and I asked to see his phone. Reluctantly, he gave it to me and while scrolling, I noticed that there hadn't been any messages in days, which was odd because we had been texting each other. I looked through random apps, one being Cashapp, and noticed he received a $150.00 payment from a woman in his training class. I asked about it and he snatched the phone from me and cussed me out like a dog. He told me it was none of my business, that I didn't need to look at that. He yelled that he didn't give me any authorization to look at that app. I stated, "I'm your wife. Why is another woman giving you money?" He stormed out of the house.

At that moment, it hit me, and I said "nope, not doing this." He came in the house regularly disrespectful to me by not speaking to me or acknowledging my life and going directly to the kids. This was so blatant to the point even the oldest noticed and asked me if we were fighting.

I was not going to do this anymore. This was not going to work for me. I could forgive the infidelity, but I would not allow him to disrespect me in front of our children. Furthermore, I would not be in a home with our children where they could see him be disrespectful to me and I just sat there, still making his plates, and packing his lunches. I'd be too through if the boys grew up and thought this was how you should treat women. The next time I saw him, I said just that and ended with, "I think it's best that we separate and get a divorce."

Nonchalantly, he said "okay."

Part 5: Time's Up

Listen, I was in a perpetual state of confusion with regard to men who were angry when they were given what they wanted. Case in point: Husband was a whole entire adulterer who, for extra razzle dazzle was also a narcissist, and refused to compromise or negotiate to make our marriage work. That alone was enough to have me consider leaving. He then became even more verbally abusive when he was home, which was rare.

I switched jobs in the midst of this foolishness and started working at an elementary school. It was nice, but the pay was awful. For extra money, I donated plasma. While heading to donate one day, my minivan was T-boned and totaled. I was unable to financially get a rental; while he had two vehicles, he was reluctant to let me drive one.

As quickly as he allowed it, a vent session I had in [what I thought was] a safe space online turned into him being told I threatened his life (I did NOT) and he no longer wanted me to drive the car. I went as far as to bring the children into the situation, asking him how they would get to and from daycare and his response was "you'll figure it out." I did: I resolved to taking public transportation. Faced with the potential responsibility of having to get the boys to and from daycare himself, he decided to allow me to continue to use one of the cars.

I was a wreck after the wreck and looked like it. I was at work in the break room when I was approached by my work mom. She said to me, "I done let you walk around this school for three days with no eyebrows and no makeup on looking crazy. What is going on with you, girl?" I immediately broke down, telling her everything, including the fact I was about to be car-less. She had lived a life and was a woman of God who had survived some cloudy days. She picked me up and got me in touch with a woman who was able to not only get me a loan with my horrible credit, but also take me to pick up my new car less than 4 days after I resolved to taking public transportation. That was God because, who else? When Husband saw the car, his response was nothing more than irritation. He looked upset that I wouldn't have to depend on him.

The next day, I said we should have a conversation about

next steps. He avoided it, and that was when he started his "present absence," as I called it. He'd be home maybe 5 or 10 minutes and he'd leave. Never would say where he was going. He would come in, grab a thing or two and leave. He would come back at whatever time in the morning he wanted to. It was crazy because he always got in our bed to sleep, not go to the couch. Some days, I would lock the room door so he couldn't. I'd have the time that he left and the time he would come back documented in my Facebook stories; he would leave 10:36PM, come back at 4:15AM. He did that for a couple of weeks.

I didn't ask where he went because I didn't care. I felt that he was doing it because he wanted to argue, and I had no fight left in me. In our last counseling session before this happened, he kept talking about me and all the things I had ever done wrong, assuming no responsibility for what he had done. Our pastor said, "Don't you realize you're the one that broke covenant? That she had her out per biblical standards and she chose to stay, yet you're still blaming her. What role did you play in any of this?" That really pissed him off, because how dare someone expect him to take accountability for anything he does, right?

He came home, pacing around and then said to me, "Okay, well, since y'all say everything is my fault, y'all tell me what you want to do." I replied, "It's not us telling you it's your fault. You are not being accountable for what you've done, nor are you understanding that healing is a process." He then said, "Well, tell me what I did that was wrong." I told him, "Honestly, if you don't see anything you did as wrong, there's nothing that any of us can tell you. Furthermore, there's no way for it to get fixed, because if you don't think anything you've done was wrong, there's a bigger problem here than what we all thought." He got mad and left like he'd been doing. I went in our room. I got on my knees, then got on my face and prayed. I cried and asked that God work this out whichever way it needed to be worked out because I couldn't handle it anymore. I asked Him to make me okay with whatever His will was for me and my babies. That was it.

About a week later we finally had a conversation about separating. I had found papers about separating online, printed them out and told him what I wanted. I told him what I thought would be fair regarding child support because the boys were young, and daycare was expensive. He responded via sticky note, *"I do not agree with your terms, and I will not be paying this amount in child support."* I wrote back, *"we need to sit down and talk about this."* He replied, *"We'll talk about it Saturday."*

Saturday came and I got the boys up and set in their room to play. I had my notebook, ready to take notes so we could try to do this as amicably as possible. As I'm talking, going through terms, I noticed that he was texting some wench on his phone. A new one at this point, and the fact that these women (using this term loosely) were just coming out of the woodworks like roaches was appalling, but I remembered who I was dealing with. I attempted to get him to interact, agree, pay attention, etc. because though it's not easy for me either, it needed to happen.

I said, "Hey, you know, this is really important. Can you please focus?"

He snarled at me and said, "Clearly, I can multitask. You can't tell me what to do. I'm paying attention."

I shook my head and continued.

Out of nowhere, he stated that he was no longer leaving the house and that the boys and I would need to move. Initially, he said that he was going to leave, yet as we're having this conversation, he's changed his mind. In my brain, I have no idea how this was going to happen. I worked for the county, I didn't make a lot of money and I could barely afford my half of the bills as it was, but I just said "Okay."

I told him the power, gas, water, and car insurance needed to be made in his name as I would be taking those things with me. He was not paying attention, but he said he was. We agreed that I would be out of the house by February 1st. Mind you, it was December, and I didn't know how this would happen, but somehow it was going to happen, right? I told him we could get this notarized to officially start the process. He left and I just sat there.

I was sad, yet I wasn't necessarily sad that the marriage was ending; I was sad because the person who stalked my favorite singer and surprised me with tickets to her show, the person I shared two beautiful boys with, the person who I shared a last name with, didn't live in that body anymore, forcing me to come to terms with reality. It hurt really bad.

To say I was stressed out trying to find a place for the boys and I would have been a gross understatement. While I was being fulfilled in work, my finances were about as depressing as my personal life. I barely bought in $2,000 a month. The only thing that I could do was lean into my village and pray. Two weeks before move out date I found a place. It was a quaint, two-bedroom, two-bathroom condo. The neighborhood looked nice, so that was where we went. I got my taxes done early so I was able to get things for the boys' room, like new beds. My room was not a priority; it was about having them impacted negatively as little as possible with this transition.

I had the exit strategy firm: when he would leave the house, I'd pack. I would put things in my trunk and cover them up, which I really didn't even need to do because he didn't touch my car. The behavior he was exhibiting was that he didn't care. I got the keys days before move-in, so I was able to take things over there. I think he really didn't think that we were going to leave. Part of me felt like he hoped I wouldn't find a place to go, so he could say I was a failure, and we would just stay there. While there was one point in life where I would have comfortably been miserable, that time had long passed.

The whole time this was in motion, I had been speaking with my sister. She and her boyfriend decided that they would come help us move. For my sister to behave like I was her archenemy and, shoot, even when I behaved like she was my archenemy, when I really needed her, she was there. I don't think I thanked her enough for what she did, which was just helping; no judgment, just loving me and the boys. We agreed to meet at IKEA and shop for some household things. We got what we needed and headed back to Greensboro, getting the apartment ready. I was really, really thankful for my sister's boyfriend who put up blinds and played with the boys. Family close by made it seem a little brighter. This experience was something that no one wants to go through and feels unfathomable until you have no choice but to fathom it.

And just like that, moving day was here. It was on a Sunday, Super Bowl Sunday to be exact. The boys and I had gone to church like always, and when we came home, Leek was getting ready for work. He got dressed, went out the door just as he always did. I waited 20 minutes and then I called everyone to come over. I could not stress enough how thankful I was for my village. About six cars pulled up and we began throwing boxes and bags wherever they could fit. I was honestly scared that he would come home in the middle of it and explode. I didn't really know what to expect, but I knew that it was time to go.

Oddly enough, while we were moving things, he texted me, stating that he had someone at work doing his taxes and he needed my social security number. I told him I was not going to give it to him and that he needed to file "Married Filing Separately." His response was filled with attitude yet again, stating that I had previously told him that he needed it. I proceeded to let him know that he was no longer going to have a wife and therefore, he wasn't getting my information. Furthermore, I was not going to allow my information to be handed over to whatever random person at his job was doing his taxes. He just stopped responding and so did I.

We may have packed that whole house up in an hour. My sister even went as far as to get all of the things out of the cabinet, which was petty but was pretty funny, actually. I left a couple of the boys' toys there because I knew that on weekends, they would be spending time with him, and I didn't want them to not have anything to play with. I made sure everything was out so that there would be no need for me to come back.

Before leaving, I took one of the dry erase boards from the kitchen and wrote him a note letting him know that as of that day, the boys and I no longer lived there, as requested. I gave him our new address, but I did not provide the apartment number. I put that board next to his alarm clock and I took a picture of it just in case he wanted to say he didn't see it, or I did not do it. Unfortunately, we had gotten to a place where I had to make sure I covered myself at all times. I had been made to feel insane and unstable far too often. No more.

Part 6: Living Single

Leaving was hard, but trying to comfort the boys, who didn't understand why they weren't seeing their father nightly, was worse. When we left, there was no contact from him for almost two weeks. When he finally did pop up to get the boys, he voiced his disdain for me, stating I turned the water and gas off unjustly (clearly, we talked about this because he said he could "multitask", remember?) and it took him time to get things back up and running. My first weekend without the boys was filled with tears. I hadn't been alone in years, and with my sunshine away, everything hit me: I was really getting divorced. What an awful reality to face, but it was mine to face.

The COVID-19 global pandemic had the world locked down shortly after our move. While wreaking havoc all over the world, I was afforded the opportunity to grieve and manage my separation in private. The days would pass, and my emotional state would be just as up in the air as that night's winning lottery numbers. One day, I woke up in the best of spirits— took time to pray and align myself with God, participated in the day's "Pray & Proverb," showered, got dressed. I got the boys up, dressed and fed; I had a protein shake because I decided to try veganism.

I grabbed everyone's bags, got coats and shoes on, locked the door, headed downstairs and somehow managed to trip and fall into The Feels. We've all been there, and there I was, unexpectedly falling on that random Wednesday. Albeit not a place you can physically see, we all go there from time to time and that day's stop actually could have been sponsored by a certain dating site telling me I was too picky and that was why I hadn't matched with anyone. (Technology will ebb and flow but it will always have the audacity.) I guess expecting a non-smoking college graduate that's at least 5'10" and believed in God was super picky. Picture that.

Being read for filth by a website algorithm did nothing more than make me feel inadequate and therefore, look to see what my ex-husband was doing. I was spying on him via social media. I have no idea why I did it. Well, that's not true. *Cue Mary J. Blige's "Not Gon Cry"* I was married to this man 3 years when I found out he had been unfaithful for 2 out of those 3 years. Unfaithful 67% of our marriage, yet repeatedly telling me how I was inadequate as a wife. There was nothing I wouldn't have done for him. I regularly state that the two blessings I birthed were products of intercourse I was not in the mood for.

I poured into his cup when my cup had been bone dry for a long time. I supported his business ventures and even created the social media accounts for them. I supported and loved two children I didn't birth, cultivating them in the face of disrespect from their mothers and never any support from him because I was doing nothing special but what I was "supposed to do." His friends and family would send thanks to me on Mother's Day before I gave birth to the boys and he legit told me, "I'll tell you Happy Mother's Day when you give birth." What in the emotional abuse is that and why did I marry it?

What Leek did was beyond my control, yet it definitely brought about insecurity. Why wasn't he grieving like I was? How could he just move someone else into what was our house, our bed, sleeping with someone on sheets I bought that our children were conceived on? Every piece of furniture in that house (with the exception of the kids' room) has remnants of Reasha on them and it was like he tried to cover me up, US up. I was HIS WIFE; was I that repulsive that he had to erase me? Good gravy; I need not to fall deeper into inception.

I had only been legally single for a few weeks, but I was already over it. The holiday season had arrived and, for the first time in 8 years, I was doing things solo. On the bright side, I only had to buy gifts for the boys now; weird because it was different. I worked so hard to get my life to the point that I could be the best example for my babies and there we were, living the exact life I didn't want for them. Yes, they would get two Christmases but let's be real: that's not what I wanted to happen. This was where my faith came in and I strived to get strength from God. I also made it a point to regularly consult my pastors because they were great, and they had been through what I was going through. They definitely gave me hope.

This was sad. From an affection perspective, I was at the point where I longed for a warm body, just to hold me. I needed admiration, care, connection. That was what made sex so great and such a desire for me. It encompassed more than just penetration; soul ties are real, and, in this context, I wanted a soul tie because I wanted that physical connection to be something between me and that man, whomever he would be. Knowing that I didn't even have access to that? Ugh, I just decided to take a vow of celibacy; not like it wouldn't be the first time for that either.

I hate it here.

An Encounter of the Hobosexual Kind

This is really all Sharlie's fault. One night while hanging out in Winston, we may or may not have partaken in an edible and decided to create Facebook Dating profiles. Judge ya mama—we're fine and gearing up to go through divorces, so we're allowed to be reckless, especially considering all children were safe and secure while the shenanigans happened. Anyway, I'm perusing the app and, in all honesty, I was bored and underwhelmed. Nothing but convicts, middle aged "rappers" and the like. And inmates; no, not felons, but currently incarcerated men who obviously have an affinity for melanin-deficient Reashas. We will definitely glance past the mid-40s day drinker (who fled the country in his 20s to avoid going to prison for fraud) that I met first because he was nowhere near as comical as who I met second.

I was minding my business one Friday morning and I got an alert that some clown, I mean, some guy, had liked me on FB Dating. This had been happening for 2 weeks almost, so I was not really concerned. I swiped and said I'd look at it later. When lunch rolled around, I logged onto Facebook, like the fiend I was, and went to see what swamp this guy came from. I clicked the tab to see and BOOM! There was a gorgeous, chiseled face looking back at me. Oh?! His name was Beetlejuice*. (I don't have time to get sued and you know what happens when you say that name and we don't need that happening. EVER AGAIN.) I scrolled through his profile with all sorts of thoughts going through my mind but in no particular order:

- Is this really him?
- This is probably some crazy foreigner trying to get my bank and Cashapp information to get the Trident gum I'm paid in, isn't it?
- Did he hit the LIKE accidentally? Because surely... (We've established I'm ridiculous so no need to dwell there.)

Anyway, messages happen, he's an actual human and we decided to exchange numbers. Cool. In my mind, I was already trying to determine how deep his voice was, I shaved about 2 inches off his height (because men height-phish regularly), but I was going to talk to him because, why not? My soon-to-be ex-husband was sowing seed all around Greensboro so that told me that was truly a done deal and since it had been 8 years, I needed to dive back into dating because I was simply too flyy to be alone. Period.

The first text message was actually a video. I opened it and he was driving (DANGEROUS) and said hi and that he just wanted to hit me up because he was thinking about me, yada yada yada. ALL THE RIGHT THINGS and obviously, I melted. Again, it had been quite some time since someone gave me any attention and it felt... nice. On top of that fact, he was gorgeous. We did the back and forth video thing and that lead to talking on the phone and COME ON sexy voice! We had a great vibe, I thought, and this was literally day 2 since we met Facebook-ally speaking.

The more we talked, the more I really liked this guy. The attraction was obvious and through conversation, there was so much energy. The type of energy that you would see in a classic rom-com. I told him about my extreme dislike for liars and how much of a turnoff dishonesty was to me. He stated he felt the same about dishonesty. He told me that while not medically diagnosed, he felt like he had a severe concussion from playing arena football and because of that, his memory was not that great and to forgive him should he repeat himself. Samesies for me, except I never played football; I just couldn't remember like I used to. Maybe liquor was to blame... anyway, FOCUS.

We were talking about religion and the Bible and he informed me that he was also married for a time and the marriage dissolved due to infidelity on his part. He allowed me into his space as he discussed his dark days and how he had evolved and became a better man, moved to North Carolina for a change of scenery and to work with children, his passion for sports and all of the things. I was all in at that point because Fixer and Helper so... new project!

I'd be remiss to point out that, for the first time in MONTHS, I noticed some activity below the Equator. Yes, my girly girl had been Harlem shaking talking to this man. It felt wrong yet right at the same time. I stood firm on my oath to myself that there would be zero sexual activity until I was no longer legally married; I was merely noting that the engine still purred. This is important because it's been all mental stimulation which is my thing, and him being easy on the eyes was a bonus.

Anyway, that Tuesday evening, we we're talking on the phone and he sounded down, so I asked about it. He told me a friend of his from back in Ohio had been going through a tough time and attempted to end his life. He noted that he previously coached this friend's son in football and shared some other information. I told him that I would pray for his friend, and he was thankful and said he'd try to contact him. Otherwise, a normal conversation.

I told him about this virtual family reunion some of my family members were having on Friday night and that I would be going to my cousin's house in Durham to take part. He got excited and asked if we could meet since he lived in Raleigh. I told him that would be cool and he said we could meet for lunch and get sushi (I love sushi). SAY LESS, sir! I was game.

We hung up, I called Sharlie (because remember, this is all her fault) and told her all about it and she was excited for me the way your friend and line sister who has unfortunately seen you at your worst can be. I got off the phone with her and passed out because it was way past my bedtime. I dreamed of him, how this date would go, the energy that would be present, all of that. In typical me fashion, I prayed that night, "God, if this isn't someone who is to mean me or my kids well, remove him and everything attached to him." Whenever I prayed prayers like that, I mean them maybe 80% of the time which is not good but it's the truth. I mean, why would a fine, caramel skinned, former semi-pro football player who's now found the Lord mean me harm in this exceptionally vulnerable state that I'm in? As if.

Fast forward a bit to Thursday. I got my hair done after work and I'm on a call with my prayer circle. I told them about this guy and how I was going to go on a date. Everyone was against it (shocker) and while I could see some logic in their thoughts, I knew I was going to go anyway. I wasn't going to be spiteful or because I didn't value their opinions; I was going because I wanted to, and I was hardheaded. Someone was always telling me not to do something, and just this once I would do it because I wanted to. I was well over 30 at this point and being sheltered wasn't something I desired to be forever. After all, it was just a date for crying out loud. I wasn't going to marry the man and pop out babies over sushi. Sheesh. I'd wake up the next day, head to Raleigh to meet him, then head to Durham for family fun. Easy peasy, lemon squeezy. Not that deep, people. Not that deep.

Fast forward a few days... it's Friday! Today is the virtual family reunion and the day I get to meet FB Dating bae. Hair is laid, I have on a beautiful dress that covers everything yet shows these boobs ever so nicely. She ready! I text him and let him know I'm headed that was early just because and I needed to know where we were meeting because I don't go to Raleigh often. I let Candice know as well because of course, I'm staying at her house.

I didn't get a reply, but it was midday, so my guess was he was working. Oh well, up the highway I go. I'm trying to calm my nerves because again, a Harlem shaking vagina can throw off sensibility; additionally, I was all too excited to be meeting someone who was a total upgrade from Maleek. This was going to be great. When I got to the Raleigh-Durham split, I decided to call him because I still had not heard from him. Straight to voicemail. That's NEVER a good sign. I'm a little nervous BUT the main point of this trip is to see my family so, if we meet, we meet and if not, not. No big deal.

I get to Candice's house, and she's gone to pick up her daughter, so I'm just driving around in the subdivision until she gets back. While I'm sitting in my car, he calls me. I answer the phone and to this day, I'm really wondering why I did that. He's on the phone sounding distraught and tells me that the "friend" he told me about 3 days prior that was contemplating suicide is actually a female, his ex-girlfriend to be exact, and that she wants to kill herself over some mess that happened in their relationship.

All facts; no printer. I'm sitting in my car in front of Candice's house flabbergasted. He's just talking and I'm quiet because what am I really going to say to this foolishness? He starts saying how sorry he is about everything and that he needs to find her and make sure she's okay and I am still very much saying nothing. I finally am able to muster words and I say to him, "Yeah, go handle that." What was I really supposed to say at that point? Be cognizant of what you pray for.

I hang up and immediately call Sharlie and I proceed to BAWL. I'm having a panic attack trying to understand why God is mad at me. Like, what did I do? I can't do anything right: I can't be married right, I can't divorce right, I can't try and date right like why am I continuously subject to malarky? Why am I subject to bull like all the time? WHY? She tries to console me but it's no use; I'm now going through what feels like the stages of grief and I tell her I'll call her back.

I muster the energy to text this man and let him know that I hate that he felt the need to be dishonest with me, to which he replies (immediately) that he wasn't dishonest about anything. I remind him that he spoke of this girlfriend like she was a man, and his response was, "I didn't specify male or female." Alrighty then, liar. I told him that I thought it was oddly convenient that the day we are scheduled to meet, hours before, that all of this allegedly takes place. He calls me on Duo. I answer but I have the phone pointed at the ground because I don't want to look at him. He then says something similar to, "You know, I don't have control over when somebody's going to say they're going to take their life. I didn't plan this and I'm sorry for the inconvenience for you, but I would rather you pray right now."

I'm still trying to understand, again, why I'm even on the phone with this fool. He then asks why the phone is pointed at the ground and why I won't look at him and I tell him he doesn't deserve to look at me and that this is a mess. I ask him where this young lady lives, and he states Holly Springs. I ask if that's in Ohio and he tells me reluctantly that it is outside Raleigh. Now it's all making sense. He tells me that the young lady is from Ohio also. He actually moved down here to be with her, but the relationship was allegedly toxic, so they broke up, but he was still paying her rent.

Mind you: this dude told me that he's been sleeping on his old roommate's couch because his lease was up and he's trying to find his own place. So, homeless but paying someone else's rent?

What is life? After I get all this information, he asks again to see me so I pick my phone up so he can see me. He looks AWFUL. Just as disheveled and distraught. He then says he still wants to see me. I'm turned off at this point but because I'm hungry (#FoodWins) I say we can meet up and Candice will tag along.

As soon as I hang up, I go to Facebook: blocked. Dating app? Blocked. Not me blocking him but he blocked ME! The audacity! I shake my head, go off with my cousin, and enjoy our night with our virtual family reunion, which was dope. The next morning, I was awakened at around 5:30 a.m. to a text from him which read,

Look what happened between us shouldn't have happened. I had a weak moment but I'm going to fight for the woman I'm still in love with. Do not call me text me or try to find me on social media.

My only response based on the lack of energy I had from the previous day was a simple: *Say less. God's grace to you both.*

I hate people.

'Twas the ever-so-eloquent Meek Mill that so wonderfully stated, "Hold up wait a minute! Y'all thought I was finished?"

About two months after this debacle and swearing off FB Dating, I chose to really try to unpack my feelings about this marriage ending and think about some missteps I made, thinking of ways to avoid repetition going forward. I didn't want to meet anymore ex-husbands and I really didn't want to meet anymore duds. My therapist is the real MVP here because I'm not in jail or hitting padded walls in an "I love me" jacket. I owe my descent back to normalcy to her helping put away luggage she didn't even pack in the first place. Yes, I know it's her job, but she did her job exceptionally well as dealing with me is truly no easy task.

One random night, after getting the boys in bed (i.e., WAR OF THE WORLDS), my phone rang, and it was an unknown number. It's election season, so I'm regularly prepared to curse people out because LEAVE ME ALONE! I know who I will be voting for and calling me repeatedly is only going to irritate me to the point of voting for the other candidate. Considering my boys are in bed, with their door closed, combined with the fact that I had yet to reach my cursing quota for the day, I answered the phone, and this is what happened:

Me: *insert irritation* HELLO!

Guy: Reasha? It's Beetlejuice.

Me: *confused because my brother doesn't live in the area code that's calling* Who?!

Guy: I know it's been a while, but I wanted to call you to sincerely apologize about what went down between us. You didn't deserve any of that. To be honest, there wasn't anyone else. The truth is, I'm homeless and I didn't want to meet you because I knew that you wouldn't want to talk to me anymore. You would have known that I was living in my car, and I just couldn't take that. It doesn't make it right that I lied, because I know you hate liars, but I didn't know what else to do. You just have everything together and I don't. I shouldn't have been on that dating site anyway and I didn't even think you would have responded to me in the first place. Anyway, I was wrong, and I totally understand if

140

you don't want to talk to me anymore, but I needed to apologize and let you know you deserve so much better."

He probably said more, but I was too busy looking at my cell phone in utter shock trying to figure out what in the April Fool's Day and Punk'd was going on here. Like, who really lies about being homeless? How are you homeless with a full-time job? What psychopathic brain creates a whole story involving suicide to mask alleged homelessness? More importantly, WHAT PLANET AM I ON THAT THIS IS EVEN HAPPENING TO ME? It's giving midlife crisis. It's giving reality tv. It's giving narcissism. Throw the whole man away.

When I put the phone back to my ear, he's checking to see if I'm still there. I inform him that, for one of very few times in my life, that I was speechless. I let him know that this was totally unexpected, and I was trying to process it. I did ask how I managed to come across his mind after this period of time and he told me he had been talking to his therapist about me. According to him, the therapist advised him to reach out to me and tell the truth to assist him on his healing journey. I have no idea who this therapist is/was and whether or not said therapist existed; I do know my therapist did not, WOULD NOT, advise me to do such a thing. Per usual, here goes my anti-smart self continuing the conversation.

It sounded sincere. To be quite honest, I cannot recall in life an instance when a man apologized to me for anything. My estranged husband never even apologized for his years' long infidelity but repeatedly stated he "made a mistake." I forgave him. Everyone is to be shown grace, right? I told him I had no true intentions of calling him ever again, yet if he were to call me, I might answer the phone. When we hung up, I was still confused as all get out, so I did what I always do— I prayed and told God to remove him if he meant me no good. After all, he did go away the first time, right?

As expected, he calls the next day and as expected, I answer. We talk and I notice there's something different about his voice. It's still him, just relaxed, happy, as if he truly could be himself after an unnecessary bout of lying for no reason. He even asked about my boys, which I thought was cool.

Things seemed okay except his jokes. They were not only awful, but they were not jokes at all. He would say things like, "I'm gonna come visit you and make a pallet on the floor like a cousin" and other weird talk. I was bothered. Like, did you forget already that you said you were homeless? He'd say things like that every day and I would repeatedly advise him that he would not be coming anywhere near my house. You are definitely not about to come squat at my spot. Absolutely NOT. Again, my fault because why am I even talking to this clown? Again, glutton for punishment.

It's now Saturday. I'm hanging out with my homegirl and talking via text to this fool. He states he's going to visit after he's done working and I say cool. He asks what the plans are, and I throw things around like grabbing food, walking around downtown, chill stuff. He says cool and he'll hit me up. I go about my business and finish with my friend then head home. At 10:34pm, whilst watching "Hamilton" for the mind-your-businessth time, he calls me saying he's about to drive to town. I advise him of the time, because there is no way he knows what time it is and still thinks I am going anywhere like it's not cold outside, especially considering he lives over an hour away. Negativo, broham. I tell him this and he says, "I can still come" and I advise him absolutely not. I don't even have pants on and I'm watching "Hamilton" which means I am not getting up and going anywhere. He gives up and I go back to watching tv. Right before tv begins to watch me, I send him a text, because I am over the shenanigans and have no idea why I thought this would be different.

I hope the next version of you I interact with is not so apprehensive about meeting me in person. Good night. Come through, passive aggression.

There was no response to that. In fact, I didn't hear from him until Monday evening. He calls and while I almost declined the call, I picked up. We exchange pleasantries and he immediately brings up Saturday. Once again, he says he consulted with his therapist about me and the interactions with me and he felt (yet again) that he needed to come clean. I have no earthly idea what

142

therapist is that readily available or who gives such advice. Furthermore, I have yet to understand to this day why a person would need to continue to feel the need to "come clean" with someone who has repeatedly stated they hate liars.

When I ask him (read, make the asinine mistake of asking him) what's up, he proceeds to tell me that he cannot see me because he can tell I am sexually frustrated. His exact words were, "when I know a woman is thirstin for a burstin,' I would feel the need to oblige, and I wouldn't want you thinking I was manipulating you."

Oh, you read that right. He did, in fact, repeat that phrase, because I just knew I was trippin and I asked him to repeat himself. "Thirstin' for a burstin'". I have officially heard it all. I begin to laugh. Hysterically. The conversation went a little something like this:

Me: "Sir, I was not going to have sex with you, nor am I trying to have sex with you. I am still legally married and—"

Him: "I've been told that before and it meant nothing."

Me: "I'm sure you have, but she ain't me. I am legally married and I'm not doing anything with anyone until that is no longer true. It does not mean the same day, next day or next year but when I am ready, so it's very bold of you to assert such a claim. Furthermore, sir, YOU ARE HOMELESS! Where would we even do it?" The nerve. To be homeless and cocky? Scandalous.

He paused for a minute, then he apologized. I wasn't really listening because I was so annoyed. I'm separated, not stupid. Soon to be divorced, not desperate. Ugh, I don't like this anymore. I don't think I really did since the first encounter went the way it did, and this second chance did not make things better.

Keep in mind, this was around day seven and this fool is out here being crazy. It's been a few months, yet active interaction may have been about 2 weeks and I still have not laid eyes on this man physically. I explained to him that I do not deal with wishy-washy people and that we both were too old to be engaging in foolishness. I wished him well and hung up the phone, with no intentions of speaking to his crazy tail again.

He would resurface one more time in January. This time, I actually met him face to face and he bought me food from Viva Chicken (FINALLY). We sat in his car, ate, and had a pretty decent conversation, but by this time I wasn't interested anymore. He kept trying to find a way to weasel himself upstairs, but I shot that down repeatedly. He also tried to kiss me, and I dodged that as well. It's amazing how someone can physically be what you want, yet on the inside be a whole jar of dumpster juice. Haven't heard from him since and I hope to keep it that way.

Epilogue

After that situation with he who will not be named, I attempted to date around a little bit more, but decided focusing more on myself would be my best bet. I did not want any baggage, residual or other, following me more than it needed to. There were times I would try to go tit-for-tat with Leek, someone who wasn't even thinking about me. I did it and had my village there to gather me when I was being crazy.

At the end of the day, healing was the best way to keep me out of a prison ministry, so healing had to happen. I spent plenty of hours in my prayer closet. I spent plenty of time at the altar at church. I spent plenty of time speaking with elders who I appreciated. They poured into me in ways I get teary-eyed thinking of. I would never say that my divorce was 100% due to infidelity; that just happened to be the straw that broke the marriage's back.

Therapy was one of the things that kept me sane during the time I spent in this valley. In November, my divorce was finalized. I got the letter in the mail and looked at it for a few minutes. It was finally official. I didn't cry; I just sat in silence, reflecting on what was and what could have been, but more, what is. Therapy was such a great thing for me during this time, with the COVID-19 pandemic offering a great assist.

One of the things that will become so real after divorce— the amount of time you think about that person is going to increase. Songs you've listened to a thousand and one times before, they now will have slight memories of that person. You could be minding your business, getting ready for bed and Alicia Keys "Never See You Again" will have you questioning life.

Show yourself grace. Remember what you have just gone through; this is someone you spent life with and that's not something that is just going to go away. Own it. You two have history. Yes, the union may be gone, but no matter how many pictures you painstakingly delete from social media, you cannot delete that part of life from happening. It did, and because of it, you have evolved into something BETTER, even though you feel as fluid as garbage juice.

It didn't seem like it at the time, but my divorce was the thing that I needed to shift my focus. My entire life I had been longing for love. Maybe it was middle child syndrome; maybe it was my father not being around— maybe it was all of that and more. I was timid in most situations, but I would force love, doing everything I could to get it. I was like a drug addict chasing a hit; I needed to have love and I didn't know where to get it. Instead of patiently figuring out ways to obtain it, I went everywhere, doing anything in hopes of getting it.

God showed me plenty of ways to get love the right way, His way, but it would take too long, and I needed it immediately. The love that I felt when I was introduced to Him was something so great that I needed to have in a tangible way. He kept telling me that wasn't the way to go. He kept telling me that I needed to change my mindset and then I could have all of the desires of my heart, but I just could not dedicate time to it.

I traveled through my own personal wilderness like the Israelites did, on a journey that could have not been the decades that it had been. A journey that could have ended in the urgency I was desperate for, but my hard head continuously landed on my soft butt, putting myself behind the wheel when I should have just sat comfortably in the passenger seat.

It's crazy that we want something so bad and when we think we have it, it doesn't look the way we thought it would, feel the way we thought it would and most of all, it doesn't last the way we thought it would. That's because we're not in charge. After all that time, all I really needed to do was look inside of me.

It didn't matter that my father wasn't there because he had his own things going on which could have impacted me in a more detrimental way. My immediate family was there, yet they weren't even aware that I was feeling the way that I felt because I didn't think I was important enough to even say anything. I had repeatedly asked God to show me where I needed to be, He would and I ignored and ignored, staying on a hamster wheel for decades and it took that wheel crashing and burning for me to finally get off of it.

That's when I knew that I had to do something different. Now, I look up. I've fallen in love again with the God who never fell out of love with me. The best part about it? I feel worthy of this love, and I feel humbled by this love.

Thankfully, there's no such thing as too late with regard to God's love. I love me so much more because I see who I am on all sides. My physical imperfections and my emotional imperfections make me perfect in His sight. This is the love that I have always been looking for and has been here the whole time. I'm thankful that He never left me, and I know that He never will. Every day is a great day because I know in Him all is well, even when it doesn't look like it. This is the love I've always wanted and the love that I've always needed. Anything else is a bonus.

I realized that as a person, not just in my marriage but in general, I made the choice to shrink myself in situations where I shouldn't have. That alone is huge because I had to truly look at my life from the start— looking different and feeling misplaced, that fight in grade school, sibling rivalry, high school, the need to feel anything but longing for love— it all encompassed me operating at a deficit and not who God created me to be.

I have a lot of talents and a lot of good in me. (I have a bit of bad also because balance.) The more time that I've spent with God, the more I learn about myself, and the fire I have for life and being a better person burns stronger and stronger as I grow closer to Him. Do I still have challenges? Of course, I'm human. I still have to manage my kids, manage their emotions and their expectations. I still expect my village to cover me and my boys, and I could not ask for a better village.

I guess you can say I'm just living proof that you can overcome what feels like the worst experience you never wanted to go through. I thought there was no better, no happy for me long-term. I was wrong. The love of Christ has allowed me the opportunity to not only love Him back, but truly, madly, deeply fall in love with who God made me, flaws and all. I was able to learn my worth and I command respect and love back.

I now choose God every chance I get because when Reasha's free will knocked her down, God's love picked her up, dusted her off, and allowed her chances to try again. No more daddy issues; no more mommy issues, sister issues, people issues. My mind and heart posture have evolved in a healthy way. Now, it's me and God, figuring this thing called life out together. It's beautiful.

As with all things, God is able to make beauty out of my ashes, and He can do that for yours, too. You do yourself a disservice sitting in complacency because you are destined for so much more. It does drizzle and downpour sometimes, but I'm here, waiting on my rainbow, because I know it's coming. God said it would, and I know it will.

About the Author

Currently southern living in the great state of North Carolina, Reasha will always be a Northerner. Born and raised in Boston, Massachusetts, she experienced the fun of growing up in the '80s & '90s while also present for a lot of life's modern upgrades. A quiet, mousy Reasha evolved into the extroverted introvert she is today; her love for writing and expression evolving with her. She is the mom of two of the best boys in the world, sister to the greatest siblings on Earth, daughter to the best mother to ever do it, and active member of the most illustrious sorority since 1920. She juggles this all while being happily involved in the best church in the Eastern Hemisphere, which, like those who are in her village know, appreciates all her dramatics.

Let's Connect!

Facebook: www.facebook.com/MyRainbowIsHere
Instagram: @MyRainbowIsHere
TikTok: @MyRainbowIsHere

www.ingramcontent.com/pod-product-compliance
Lightning Source LLC
Chambersburg PA
CBHW051205120626
46547CB00013B/1209